The Message of Genesis

RALPH H. ELLIOTT

The Message of Genesis

BROADMAN PRESS
Nashville, Tennessee

© 1961 • BROADMAN PRESS
Nashville, Tennessee

421-06252

Library of Congress catalog card number: 61-7547

Printed in the United States of America
4.D6013

To
my wife
Virginia
my daughters
Jenny
Bev

Preface

Various types of mining operations have been conducted in the book of Genesis. Often these have been responsible for the obliteration of what the book actually has to say to the heart and mind of man. Sometimes this has happened because the interpreter failed to take advantage of the best in the field of Old Testament scholarship and criticism. The scholar, in his quest for objectivity, has erred at times in the other direction by forgetting the religious factor involved in interpretation. The present work is an effort to combine head and heart by using the sound achievements of modern scholarship to ferret out and to underscore the foundational theological and religious principles of the stories of Genesis.

It is assumed that the reader is familiar with the content itself; little time thus will be spent in retelling the story. It is hoped that the reader will turn directly to the Bible for needed prodding in this area. There will be a probing for the purpose for which the story or passage has been included in the Scriptures. The objective is to find the meaning or message of Genesis.

To best accomplish this task, three divisions are needed in the work. Although Part I is related to the consideration of the Pentateuch as a whole, it outlines and develops a method of approach without which the writer particularly feels that a correct understanding of Genesis is impossible. Since chapters 1-11 in themselves have a distinct purpose and mission of a preparatory nature, it is fitting that they should constitute Part II, with chapters 12-50 forming Part III.

Part I outlines the methodological perspectives of the author. This is necessary in order to appraise accurately the body of the theological interpretation. Readers not interested in the technical aspects of the material may want to go more directly to the sections dealing with interpretation.

A striking difference of style will be noticed in the author's consideration of chapters 1-11 and his treatment of chapters 12-50. This is necessitated by the very nature of Genesis. Problems of interpretation are much more perplexing, detailed, and involved in the first eleven chapters.

Though the material in this book is mine, and I do not wish anyone else to be charged with its deficiencies, I do wish to express my appreciation to Dr. Clyde T. Francisco, my teacher and later a colleague on the faculty of Southern Baptist Theological Seminary, Louisville, Kentucky. It was in an elective course in the Pentateuch under his guidance that I first gained inspiration and purpose to attempt a serious study of the book of Genesis. Thus, I am sure that many of the insights which culminated in my own mind were placed there in seed-bed fashion by him. A similar debt is owed to Dr. J. J. Owens, who gave me facility in the Hebrew language; and to Dr. William Morton who, through the eyes of archaeology, gave me a dynamic appreciation for the nature of the biblical revelation.

My student secretaries, Eldridge Fleming and Duane Willard, have typed, worked, encouraged, and applauded. I shall never forget their warm fellowship and help. Long-time friend and now associate, Dr. Roy Lee Honeycutt, patiently read the manuscript and gave his helpful appraisal.

Finally, I cannot express sufficient gratitude to Dr. Millard J. Berquist, president of Midwestern Baptist Theological Seminary, who has provided such a wonderful environment in which to work and who has been friend and champion in the pursuit of our common task.

RALPH H. ELLIOTT

Contents

Authorship and Date

Appreciation of Importance

Much time and labor would be saved if one could accept the late-inserted superscription of most translations—"The First Book of Moses, Commonly Called Genesis." However, to do so would be to ignore the fact that the name of Moses does not occur in the Hebrew text. It was first used in the Septuagint, or Greek translation.[1] The title bears no ancient authority, and concentrated efforts have been directed to the question of authorship for hundreds of years. The question was considered by such early church fathers as Origen and was prominent in the thought of the Jewish rabbis of the Middle Ages, such as Abraham Ibn Ezra (1088-1167). There continues to be much active study in this area, and today only a few people seek to justify Mosaic authorship for the entire body of material.

The question is not an empty one. It is impossible to interpret a biblical book properly unless something is known about the historical situation, the general cultural milieu, the religious environment, and the needs out of which the material was born. Literature is not born in a vacuum, and this is true of biblical as well as other writing. Such was the emphasis of the early twentieth-century German scholar, Gunkel, in his *Gattungen* (forms of literature) and in his stress upon *Sitz im Leben* (setting in life). In addition to the importance

---

[1]John Skinner, *A Critical and Exegetical Commentary on Genesis*, Vol. I of *The International Critical Commentaries*, ed. Samuel Driver, Alfred Plummer, and Charles Briggs (Edinburgh: T. & T. Clark, 1910), p. i.

1

of the historical setting, the understanding of which creates an atmosphere for interpretation, there are several problem spots in Genesis which make the question of authorship and date one of paramount importance.

Notice some problems related to authorship. Many of these will have to be faced with more detailed scrutiny in the actual discussion of Genesis 1-50. First, there are the so-called "duplicate accounts"; more than one account of the same event frequently occurs. At times this may be the mere repetition for emphasis' sake or perhaps the presentation of different phases of the story under varying circumstances. However, at times these accounts seem to come from different authors, even as the Gospel writers have varying accounts and perspectives.

One of the most striking repetitions in Genesis is the double account of creation. Genesis 1:1 to 2:3 gives the order of creation with man appearing as the last and crowning act of creation, male and female being created together. Genesis 2:4-25 presents man as the first creature, with the garden in which to place him appearing afterward. Man and woman appear in separate order. Several duplicates appear in the Abrahamic narratives. Twice Abraham represents his wife as his sister (12:10-20; 20:1-18); three times he receives the promise of a son (15:4; 17:16; 18:10); more than once Isaac's name is explained as meaning "he laughs" (17:17-19; 18:12-13; 21:6); twice Hagar is expelled from Abraham's household because of Sarah's jealousy (16:4-14; 21:9-21). More complicated than any of these is the delicate question of various sets of instructions given to Noah, such as to take into the ark one pair of each kind of animal (6:19 f.) and, again, to use seven pairs of each clean beast and one pair each of unclean beasts (7:2 f.)

While duplicate accounts do not conclusively prove more than one author, they are so suggestive as to indicate the possibility that one may be dealing, not simply with one author, but with accounts from various authors or traditions woven together.

Certain anachronisms occur—statements more consistent with a later date than with the time of Moses. Joseph said that he was stolen out of "the land of the Hebrews" (40:15), but at the time of Joseph and of Moses, Palestine was known as the land of Canaan, not as the land of the Hebrews. Similar is the phrase "land of the Philistines" (21:34; 26:1); the Philistines did not get into Palestine until about 1150 B.C. Obviously there is an anachronism here.

Of serious concern are some chronological references in the book which have a disturbing character. Genesis 12:6 and 13:7 both speak of the Canaanites as "then" being in the land. This would imply that at the time of writing Canaanites were no longer present. However, they were still there when Moses was alive. This immediately suggests that Moses was not the author of this material. Reference is made in 36:31 to the kings that reigned over Edom before there reigned a king over Israel. This portion of the writing seems late, at least as late as the time of the monarchy. The only alternative is to disregard the historical setting and suggest that the writer anticipated that the Jews would have a king at some later date.

Contributions of Literary Criticism

To notice such divergencies as have been presented is to recognize one's debt to literary criticism, the effort to find and evaluate the historical context, locale, identity, and intended usage of any writer and his writings.

Early among those interested in a more serious study of the Pentateuch, of which Genesis is a part, was the famous Bishop of Lyons, Irenaeus. Born A.D. 130, he dedicated his life to the exposure of various heresies in a quest for true faith. His principal writing, *Against Heresies,* exposed and refuted the gnostic heresy. Yet, in spite of his defense of orthodoxy, he questioned the Mosaic authorship of the Pentateuch. Continued consideration of the question was given by Celsus, Clement of Alexandria, Origen, Tertullian, Jerome, and a host of others. Beginning early in the Christian era, an effort to understand the Old Testament thus necessitated a study of the problem of authorship. It should not be surprising that the question has remained alive through the ages and that various conclusions have been reached.

Though his work reaped no immediate result, Ibn Ezra (1088-1167), famous Jewish scholar and careful student of the Hebrew Scriptures, entertained serious doubt about the Mosaic authorship of Genesis 12:6 and Genesis 22:14. Both passages have points of anachronistic or chronological difficulty. Questions present in germ fashion in the Middle Ages burst to life in the period of free inquiry beginning with the Reformation.

A. B. Carlstadt, pioneer reformer, emphasized many of the basic principles on which Martin Luther later stood. He and Luther both felt that non-Mosaic authorship was not a matter of such serious proportions as to discredit the Scriptures. Catholic scholars of the same period, such as A. Masius (Du Maes) in 1574, had serious questions because of the anachronistic naming of cities such as Dan (Gen. 14:14) and Hebron (Gen. 13:18; 23:2). These names did not properly belong to the cities of Laish and Kirjatharba until after the death of Moses.

In 1670 Spinoza, a Portuguese Jew living in Holland, expressed his views concerning the Old Testament in a work, *Tractatus Theologico-Politicus*. Because of his study of such questions as the anachronism of Genesis 12:6, he eventually suggested that a mass of ancient documents lay in the background to the composition of the pentateuchal books, such as Genesis, and that perhaps they had been compiled and pulled together in their present form by Ezra.

About the same time, in 1678, Father Richard Simon, a

French priest, wrote his views in *A Critical History of the Old Testament*. He suggested that Moses wrote many documents but that the bulk of the Pentateuch was finished later, perhaps on the basis of these documents. With reference to Genesis, Simon recognized three factors: (1) diversity in the two creation stories, (2) possibility of separating the narrative of Genesis into two complete accounts, (3) the two stories of the Flood.

Though usually not noticed, some of the most significant work of the early period was done by Heuning Bernhard Witter, a German pastor. In 1753 he drew attention to the alternation of divine names in Genesis, the presence of doublets, and differences in style. On this basis, he carried through an analysis of Genesis and the first two chapters of Exodus. Though he did not deny Mosaic authorship, he did suggest that Moses had used earlier documents as his sources.

The work which led to the modern period of Genesis study, and really to all major Old Testament critical study, was that of a lay theologian, Dr. Jean Astruc. Astruc was a French medical doctor assigned as the court physician of Louis XV of France; he also served as a professor of medicine at the University of Paris. He made a study of the Pentateuch in an effort to discover some dietary principles which might help the king's digestive system. As he studied, he noticed that two names were generally used for God—Yahweh and Elohim. He decided to place material using the name Yahweh in one column and that using the name Elohim in another. To his surprise, this action made two continuous narratives which told approximately the same story.

Similar to Witter, Astruc regarded the divergent material as different authors' notes which had been pieced together by Moses. His conclusion involved three basic assumptions: (1) Moses had written the book of Genesis through the use of two basic sources, one using "Elohim" and the other using "Yahweh"; (2) in addition to the two basic ones, nine or ten other sources were used; (3) Moses had copied the material into four parallel columns which were later confused, causing a mixing of the documents. Some of the difficulties in our present text resulted.

Astruc's work was the foundation for that of the "father of higher criticism," J. G. Eichhorn, who in 1779 published a three-volume *Introduction to the Old Testament.* He gathered together the work of Simon and Astruc and analyzed the book of Genesis, listing the characteristics of style in the two narratives which Astruc had found. He also noted that other passages—such as the narrative of the invasion of the four kings in Genesis 14, and the blessing of Jacob, Genesis 49:1-27—did not seem to fit into the basic pattern of two narratives. He thus concluded that many fragments had completed and complemented the two basic sources. The basic sources are commonly called J (after the German spelling of Yahweh) and E.

Karl David Ilgen (1798), Eichhorn's successor at the University of Jena, and Hermann Hupfeld (1853), a learned grammarian and professor at the University of Halle, both noted that the E material seemed to be variant in nature. They singled out a part of it that is characterized by an emphasis on ceremony, ritual, and exactness. It was thought that this was the work of a priestly group, and so three sources—J, E, and P—were suggested.

In 1805 a doctoral student at the University of Jena, Wilhelm DeWette, wrote a graduate treatise on Deuteronomy. He assigned much of the material of Deuteronomy to the seventh century. From that day to this, the "documentary hypothesis"—in recognizing the four sources J, E, P, and D— has been prominent in Old Testament study. Only J, E, and P are regarded as sources of Genesis.

Lacking a popularizer, this work might have passed into oblivion. However, Julius Wellhausen in his 1878 *Prolegomena to the History of Israel* so developed and popularized the documentary hypothesis that it became basic in the Old Testament study of both Europe and America. Nonetheless, much of Wellhausen's work was negative in tone.

With reference to the book of Genesis, Wellhausen's study added little information. Though successful in analyzing various parts of the Pentateuch and in tracing the historical development of institutions, Wellhausen failed to see the meaning of the books as a whole as they now appear. His basic fallacy was the supposition that Israel's religion had to be no better than the culture out of which it came. The significance of revealed religion was minimized. In spite of all that has been said, however, Wellhausen's dating of the documents (850, 750, 621, and 500 B.C.), and his work in acquainting the world with the literary critical method were milestones in Old Testament study.

Modifications of Oral Tradition

Adherents to the documentary hypothesis believe that the basic material of Genesis was written in the three general periods of the eighth, seventh, and sixth centuries. Correctness of the dating, of course, is a distinct matter from recognition of the sources. But it is in dating that the limitations of the literary critical school loom large. Though a document or tradition or stratum used in the structure of Genesis might not have been written until the eighth, seventh, or sixth centuries, it might contain material passed on for centuries through oral tradition before being written down.

Debt for such insight is due primarily to Hermann Gunkel (1862-1932), who directed attention to the study of the "forms" (*Gattungen*) of literature and to the "situation in life" (*Sitz im Leben*). By studying the forms of literature comprising the documents, one can find out that the individual units are quite old, even though the completed document might be of more recent origin. In addition, Gunkel was able to initiate an emphasis which Wellhausen had missed. Though

Genesis, as well as other Old Testament books, reflects the culture and environment from which it had borrowed, these borrowed elements were placed in a new context, "baptized" so to speak. They became vehicles for insights and teachings which were distinctively different from the original settings of the material. Thus, as Eduard Nielsen has said so strikingly:

If one admits that a written source, the literary age of which is three or four hundred years younger than that of another, contains features that are considerably older than the recension of the oldest written source, then one presupposes—as Gunkel does too,—that these written sources are the reduction to writing of century-old traditions, where the time of the reduction to writing in reality says nothing as to the age of the material, but at most something about its last revision. This is a very fruitful point of view, but at the same time it deprives literary criticism of one of its favourite criteria. For according to this view it is impossible as a matter of course to divide the material into three age groups and to distribute the three groups among J, E, and P. For here indeed the youngest source has an element which is older than the present form of the oldest source.[2]

Gunkel worked primarily with the book of Genesis and tried to identify the material that had been handed down by oral tradition and the part that had been written to tie the traditions together. Much of the material of Genesis may have been gradually collected over a period of centuries at particular worship centers until finally certain emphases became characteristic of various sections of the country. Perhaps there were four major worship centers. What was characteristic of these four worship centers may constitute what came to be written down as four documents.

Consequently, Genesis is not to be considered as composed of three documents which a man or men simply sat down and wrote at one sitting. These documents, when finally written,

---

[2] Eduard Nielsen, *Oral Tradition* (Chicago: Alec R. Allenson, Inc., 1954), pp. 96-97.

were composed of strata of many different periods of Israel's history. It follows then that each stratum of material contains much which is parallel to another stratum. It should be expected that each stratum would have some pre-exilic and some postexilic material. All strata apparently go back to a common source, although they branched off in different directions and were shaped according to the imprint of each individual locale.

This line of research has continued in more recent years under the direction of the so-called Scandinavian or Uppsala school, identified with the University of Uppsala in Sweden. Though built upon the initial effort of Gunkel, this approach was sparked by H. S. Nyberg of the Swedish school. In 1935 his book *Studien zum Hoseabuche*[3] suggested that the Hebrew text of the Old Testament is dependent on an oral tradition that was thoroughly trustworthy, the chief means of the preservation of material before the Exile. Reinforcing what has been suggested, Bentzen wrote:

The historical importance of this for the Old Testament is of course apparent. Only on this presupposition of the importance of oral transmission can it be understood that the literature of the Old Testament from pre-exilic days survived the crisis of the *Babylonian Exile*. The priests, the disciples of prophets, and the sages can scarcely have been allowed to carry much more luggage with them in the long deportation columns of 587 than let us say Poles or Jews deported by the Nazis in our times, or Armenians in the Turkish transports 30 years ago. Manuscripts or clay tablets "incidentally" saved would certainly have had to be supplemented by living oral tradition. A later generation considered it a miracle that the Law could have been restored after the burning of the temple. The author of 4 Ezra believes that it was due to Divine Inspiration that *Ezra* was enabled to rewrite the Law.[4]

---

[3]H. S. Nyberg, *Studien zum Hoseabuche, Zugleich ein Beitrag zur Klaerung des Problems der Altestamentlichen Textkritik* (Uppsala Universitets Arsskritt, 1935).

[4]Aage Bentzen, *Introduction to the Old Testament* (2d ed.; Copenhagen: G. E. C. Gads Forlag, 1952), I, 104.

Numerous evidences of the use of oral tradition are to be found in the Scriptures. Though there are no specific statements that the principle was followed with reference to Genesis, there is no reason to suppose that the procedure here differed from that used elsewhere. Specific directions for the preservation of tradition are to be found in Exodus 17:14; Deuteronomy 31:19 f.; Joshua 10:13; Habakkuk 2:2. For convincing evidence that oral tradition has assumed an important place in the transmission not only of the literature of the Old Testament but of all cultures, see the splendid treatment by Eduard Nielsen in the monograph *Oral Tradition* of the "Studies in Biblical Theology" series.

Specifically, as applied to Genesis and other books of the Pentateuch, Murtonen has done a marvelous job in giving evidence that the J and E material was written down quite early. His study is based on the generally accepted principle that the use of *matres lectionis*[5] increases as one passes from older writings to younger ones.[6] Thus he writes:

If we leave D out of account for the present, the fixation in writing of the other parts of the Pentateuch seems to have followed in the following order:
(1) Decalogue
(2) Stories of E of the period before Exodus
(3) The laws of Numbers 15:4
(4) The stories of E of the fathers
(5) The story of Exodus, etc. in J
(6) The book of Covenant and Numbers 28-30
(7) The Holiness Code
     P story of the fathers
     E story of Jethro's visit
     the laws incorporated in P[7]

---

[5]Early Hebrew had no vowels. *Matres lectionis* were certain consonants (י, ו, ה, א) used to indicate vowel sounds.

[6]A. Murtonen, "The Fixation in Writing of Various Parts of the Pentateuch," *Vetus Testamentum*, III (1953), 46-53.

[7]*Ibid.*

In view of the foregoing, it must be admitted that no specific author and date can be given for Genesis. As will be noted later, when effort is made to interpret the creation stories, some of the material has roots going back to the early Sumerian-Babylonian period (3000-1500 B.C.). The form of its application to divine history perhaps is exilic and postexilic (500 B.C.). Many human authors, worship circles,[8] and redactors[9] appear to have had a part in shaping Genesis over a long period of time. In a special sense, this underscores the fact that God is the ultimate author. In his wisdom, providence, and persuasion, he revealed to the hearts of many generations the story of man's need and God's answer. This approach to Genesis—the belief that the sovereign God could speak the message consistently and have it comprehended through many human instruments—spells *miracle*. Many circles molded, adapted, and modified the material to meet the crises in life and worship in their own day. Nevertheless, the thread of the divine guided and engineered its final culmination in lasting religious principles applicable to any age and to any society.

General Nature of Revelation

From what has been said, something of the author's understanding of the nature of the biblical revelation should have been ascertained. It is only fair that the reader be aware of the suppositions which guide a particular interpretation.

John Wick Bowman, in the 1951 Sprunt lectures at Union Theological Seminary in Virginia, pointed to what he called "prophetic realism" in biblical interpretation. He defines "prophetic realism" or the "dialogue of reason" as "a dialogue between God and man—a dialogue of such an intimate nature that man *within history* really comes to know God and to pur-

---

[8]A worship circle or ritual is usually called a cult in Old Testament scholarship.

[9]A redactor was an editor who arranged and revised the basic sources from which the Pentateuch was composed.

pose to do his will."[10] This seems to be the secret of the biblical revelation.

The Bible is the theological or religious record of God's dealing with man in history! The historical situation in which the Hebrews lived provided a crisis and a need. The Bible is an account of how God met that need.

Whether it be in Genesis or elsewhere, the account of how the need was met provides the true principles of religion through which God still breathes and which he uses as the basis of *continuing* to reveal himself. For this reason, S. H. Hooke is right when he suggests that as one attempts to study the Scriptures, three levels must be kept in mind.

What Hooke calls "the level of historical event"[11] indicates that something happened. The interpreter's task is thus to discover the nucleus and basic content of history underlying the story. The Hebrews knew that something had happened which made things radically different. When any period of stress or doubt came, they always went back to that special history. For example, Voegelin directs attention to Psalm 136, a "drama of Israelite history," where one sees depicted "the process from the creative solitude of God to its completion through the establishment of the servants of Yahweh in the land of promise."[12]

But there must be also a "level of interpretation."[13] As Hooke suggests, this level has to do with "those who participated in the events and those who, later on, reflected on the traditions, oral or written, of the events, interpreted them in terms of the divine activity and purpose as it concerned themselves and their people."[14] It is right to recognize that in

---

[10]John Wick Bowman, *Prophetic Realism and the Gospel* (Philadelphia: Westminster Press, 1945), pp. 41 f. (italics added).

[11]S. H. Hooke, *The Siege Perilous* (London: Student Christian Movement Press, Ltd., 1956), p. 224.

[12]Eric Voegelin, *Israel and Revelation* ("Order and History," Vol. I, Baton Rouge: La. State University Press, 1956), p. 135.

[13]Hooke, *loc. cit.*

[14]*Ibid.*

God's act of revelation, the interpretation was controlled by the horizon or mental climate of the time and might be modified in the light of a fuller knowledge of God or in a better comprehension of God's revelation.[15]

Creation was event; the lives of the patriarchs constituted event. It was for succeeding generations, however, to translate these events into meaning as they analyzed the event and as they comprehended God. Consequently, it would be somewhat immature to deny that religious understandings and conceptions underwent change. This does not mean that the people who gave Genesis to the world merely comprehended everything on the level of their own lives and minds. It does mean that the basic thought modes of the day were used to express a higher, inner, and more spiritual comprehension. They interpreted everything through the realization that they were vitally related to God through faith and that they must keep that relationship clear. They lived with what Eric Voegelin has called the Hebrew "Leap in Being."[16] This means that Israel was not, contrary to Auguste Comte, simply restricted to knowledge derived from natural phenomena.

Summarizing the two levels thus far presented, this is to say that neither the book of Genesis nor the Bible as a whole is basically a compilation of intellectual propositions or concepts handed down to man. One very vital concept is that "God is love." However, had God simply said to a man one day, "Now write this down for all to read: 'God loves you,'" it is doubtful that many ever would have been impressed by the reading of that concept. Man knows, believes, and lives by the fact that God loves us because something happened in history to demonstrate his love. The Bible is, thus, a report

---

[15]*Ibid.* This important principle was recognized by John Calvin, who attributed it to God's voluntary accommodation of himself to the limits of human understanding; cf. Edward A. Dowey, Jr., *The Knowledge of God in Calvin's Theology* (New York: Columbia University Press, 1952), pp. 3 ff.

[16]Voegelin, *op. cit.*, p. 14.

and an interpretation of events through man in his cultural milieu and background. Emil Brunner suggests that this word of God in the Old Testament is not something audibly heard. It is the "breaking in" from the divine world into the world of man—whether through thunder, earthquake, wind, or fire, but in such a way as man understands that this is a manifestation, a sign, or "word" from God.[17]

Floyd Filson, in his 1950 presidential address to the Society of Biblical Literature, was emphasizing the same tenet when he said that "the revelation . . . was not the detached disclosure of ideas, but the self-disclosure of God in specific occurrences and through the actions of chosen spokesmen."[18]

Genesis is to be approached with the belief that revelation means God's disclosing himself in mighty acts for salvation. Suppose that a biblical writer should now or then use poor grammar, poor science, or even poor history in reporting God's act. The important thing is the fact that the divinely inspired writer presents the act itself with clarity and truth. Error in literary vehicle does not necessarily mean error in message or in the essential purpose of God.[19]

To say what has been said is to say with Hooke that there is a third element which absolutely must not be forgotten. This is the "level of the divine activity itself." This transcends both the historical event itself and the interpretation. As the book is used today, "we no longer see the revelation πολυμερῶς καὶ πολυτρόπως (in many ways at various times), but as a whole, from the first glory of creation to the final glory of redemption, summed up in the Son."[20] While it is important to keep hold of the fact that God acts in history, it is even

---

[17]Emil Brunner, *Revelation and Reason*, trans. Olive Wyon (London: Student Christian Movement Press, Ltd., 1947), p. 86.

[18]Floyd Filson, "Method in Studying Biblical History," *Journal of Biblical Literature*, LXIX (March, 1950), 2.

[19]H. Cunliffe-Jones, *The Authority of the Biblical Revelation* (London: James Clarke & Co., Ltd., 1945), pp. 29-31.

[20]Hooke, *op. cit.*, p. 224.

more important to remember that the significance of God's act is never exhausted by the immediate historical situation in which it takes place.[21] The Holy Spirit breathes over the pages, and thus this redemptive act of salvation quickens the reader's heart to know God. This is the "level of divine activity."

Suffice it to say that Genesis will be approached from a theological-religious standpoint. Attention will be given to the sources, but too much shallowness has transpired in the past by simply looking at the sources. Critical study must be, not an end in itself, but a tool to help us go from the basic historical situation to a positive theological emphasis which challenges the people of one's own day.

In other words, one must come to the place that he sees the parabolic and symbolic nature of much of the Old Testament Scriptures. Genesis is to be understood in this light. It is not science. In the material attributed to J and P, the early writers were in no way trying to give a scientific or literal explanation. These stories are what Alan Richardson called parables—"parables of nature and man in order to convey deep religious insight."[22] Since the parable includes the historical and the nonhistorical, one can say with Richardson:

We must learn to think of the stories of Genesis—the Creation, the Fall, Noah's ark, the Tower of Babel . . . in the same way as we think of the parables of Jesus; they are profoundly symbolical (though not allegorical) stories, which aren't to be taken as literally true (like the words of the textbook of geology), but which yet bear a meaning that cannot be paraphrased or stated in any other way without losing something of their quality of existential truth.[23]

---

[21]*Ibid.*, p. 226.
[22]Alan Richardson, *Genesis I-XI* (London: Student Christian Movement Press, Ltd., 1953), p. 18.
[23]*Ibid.*, p. 19.

Quite a different approach must be used when the journey is begun at chapter 12, for the patriarchs are to be treated as historical personages with a chronicle of events which actually happened in daily life. But even here there is an element over and beyond historicity, for the purpose of putting the stories "on record" is to interpret a meaning which is not seen in bare event itself. Here again one faces the "level of interpretation" and the "level of divine activity."

Finally, criticism has an important place in underscoring the biblical view of history and revelation, but critical study must be built "into the life of faith as an integral and constructive factor and thereby to regain for the student's life the fundamental unity which a false standard of objectivity has tended to destroy."[24]

---

[24]Filson, *op. cit.*, p. 18.

Part II

The Need of Man

General Introduction

It is generally helpful to know how things started, and so the first book of the Bible sets out to tell us just that—the beginning of things. This not only describes the content of the book but it is also the reason for its name. Genesis, the name by which the book is generally called, is transliterated from the Greek (Septuagint) translation γένεσις, which means "source, origin, ancestry, or birth." However, according to the custom of naming a book after the first word or phrase of the book, the Hebrews even more correctly refer to it as "In Beginning," after the Hebrew בְּרֵאשִׁית, the first word.

Genesis, or "In Beginning," is a good name, for the book tells the beginnings of all things connected with faith. The blueprint of theology is the book of Genesis. As suggested by Dr. John R. Sampey, herein is told the beginning of the material universe.[1] However, it must be remembered that the book is interested in the beginning of the universe because of its religious value and its stress upon the sovereignty of God. Genesis does not emphasize matters of a scientific nature. As the ecclesiastical historian of the sixteenth century, Cardinal Baronius is reported to have suggested, "The intention of Holy Scripture is to teach us how to go to heaven, and not how the heavens go."[2] Likewise, reported here is the arrival of man, sin's characteristic entrance into the world, the

---

[1]John R. Sampey, *The Heart of the Old Testament* (Nashville: Broadman Press, 1922), pp. 15 ff.
[2]*Ibid.*, p. 15.

17

beginning of a redemptive plan, the inauguration of the Hebrew people and patriarchal society as a medium of fostering the plan, and the beginning of institutional life as seen in the sabbath.

Though there is no stated purpose within the book itself, the name is indicative of the general purpose of the book— to trace the beginnings of redemptive history. This is the larger purpose, or as another has put it, its purpose is to portray "generation, degeneration, and regeneration."[3] It is an introduction to the story of redemption, which reaches its climax in the New Testament revelation and continues even to the present moment. Genesis, thus, is a religious book; it is designed as a "theological history" to show the origin of things— not from a detailed, factual, scientific standpoint, but from a theological standpoint. It is just at this point that past difficulty often developed in considering Genesis. By a happy turn of events, recent scholarship emphasizes the meaning and message; for in its present form Genesis is essentially a theological book.

Minute study is not the purpose at this point; rather, the purpose here is to bolster the argument of the theological nature of the book. A hurried survey here will give perspective for detailed discussion at the proper time. The plight of man and his need for redemption are portrayed in Genesis 1-11. These chapters form a theological preface to the remainder of the book. Various emphases are then made in order to show the intensity of sin which characterizes the life of every man.

As a setting for the drama, chapters 1-3 have to do with man and the universe. Two creation stories are presented, not because the compiler failed to harmonize his sources, but because he wished to give a twofold emphasis. The first creation story, chapter 1, has to do with the *power* of God

---

[3]W. H. Griffith Thomas, *Through the Pentateuch Chapter by Chapter* (Grand Rapids: Wm. B. Eerdman's Publishing Co., 1957), p. 28.

behind creation, while the story in chapter 2 emphasizes the *intended fellowship* between God and man. Concluding this section, chapter 3 shows in the life of every man the sin which causes separation from God and the resultant disharmony to the entire created order.

Chapters 4 and 5 emphasize the fact that man does not keep his sin to himself but spreads it to all civilization and all society. Sin has sociological implications. Something of a climax is reached in 6:1 to 11:25; there the note is judgment because of the sin which characteristically infects all mankind. Added to the picture of judgment symbolized by the Flood is the table of nations in chapter 10. Its purpose, much like that of chapter 3, is to suggest that even as sin characterizes every man, so judgment must touch every man. This is implemented by the tower of Babel account in chapter 11.

With every picture of darkness there is a contrasting picture of light, and so in Genesis 12-50 there is initiated an answer to the plight of man. Indeed, chapters 12-50 are concerned with soteriology. Following a glimpse of the initiation of God's plan of redemption through a people (12-24) are the Jacob stories, whose underlying purpose is to show man's feebleness in God's plan (25-36). There is a concluding note in the Joseph stories, which shows, in spite of man's feebleness, God's perseverance and providence in his plan (37-50).

Thus, one sees that the book of Genesis is not a scientific textbook or even a detailed historical picture of actions and events. It is really a blueprint for theology. Questions of science and history are important; but the most essential questions are not whether Genesis 1 can be harmonized with geology and biology, whether Abraham accurately represents the customs of the day, or whether the trees in the garden are literal or figurative. The primary aim is seeing what the book has to tell about the revelation of God to the needs of men.

Theological understanding of Genesis brings a note of assurance to the human heart, disproving false theology. As

stressed by H. Wheeler Robinson, Genesis sounds a death
blow to deism, dualism, and pantheism.[4] Dr. John R. Sampey
caught the same picture when he paraphrased Murphy to the
recognition that Genesis denies atheism, for it assumes the
being of God; it disclaims polytheism, for it confesses the one
eternal Creator; it denies materialism, for it asserts the creation
of matter and shows that man is closer to the spiritual than
he is to the material; and it denies pantheism, for it assumes
the existence of God before all things.[5]

Careful literary artistry complements the theological melody
of the book. Genesis was carefully planned, the author having
given it an introduction and ten major headings. The term
תּוֹלְדוֹת (*toledoth*), meaning "generations," occurs as a
heading to each of the ten sections of the book, and each of
these ten sections is based around the generations of important
people. The root *yaladth*, to beget, be born, to have history,
or to have descendants, is behind the word. One does not
have to labor to make an outline. The author's insertion of
toledoth naturally divides the material as follows:

Introduction: The Creation Account, 1:1 to 2:3
I. The History of Heaven and Earth, 2:4 to 4:26
II. The History of Adam, 5:1 to 6:8
III. The History of Noah, 6:9 to 9:29
IV. The History of the Sons of Noah, 10:1 to 11:9
V. The History of Shem, 11:10-26
VI. The History of Terah, 11:27 to 25:11
VII. The History of Ishmael, 25:12-18
VIII. The History of Isaac, 25:19 to 35:29
IX. The History of Esau, 36
X. The History of Jacob, 37:2 to 50:26

Although *toledoth* appears in these ten sections, three appearances are basic. The initiation of concern is to be seen

---

[4]H. Wheeler Robinson, *Inspiration and Revelation in the Old Testament*
(Oxford: Clarendon Press, 1946), p. 21.

[5]Sampey, *op. cit.*, pp. 14-15.

in Adam, in whom the race is thought to be born; continuation is met in Noah, in whom the race is preserved; and preservation is stressed through Abraham, in whom the race was blessed.[6]

No detailed information about time is given, and no dates are to be found. Questions of age and time are for speculation and for scientific research. This is in keeping with the general purpose which has already been stressed. The emphasis is not on how the world came into existence, in the sense of intricate analysis, but that it did come into being and that God was behind it all.

For scientific information, go to science. There will be no conflict between theological truth and scientific truth. Simply stated, Genesis deals with matters beyond the scope of science —man's awareness of his existence in the presence of God and his dependence upon, and responsibility toward, God. Its prime purpose is to present theological truth.

Part II has to do with that portion of the drama which concerns the history of the world and man prior to Abraham. It is an effort to show the nature of God's dealing with man and the principles underlying that relationship of God and man everywhere. It is the preface showing the necessity for a plan and process of redemption which begins with Abraham.

Both Priestly and Yahwistic materials comprise the section. The Priestly parts are: the cosmogony (1 to 2:4a); the list of patriarchs from Adam to Noah (5:1-32); an account of the Flood (6:9 to 9:29); a table of people (10:1-32); the genealogies of Shem (11:10-26) and Terah (11:27-32), ending with Abraham.

The remainder of the material belongs to J. Only two features, the creation and the Flood, are given in detail by P. This is significant, for these are two of the four world ages which are found in the Priestly material; and in these are two of the four institutional emphases which are made. From the

---

[6]Thomas, *op. cit.*, p. 29.

creation to the Flood appears the sabbath; the period from
Noah to Abraham is marked by the sanctity of blood; the
time from Abraham to Moses is marked by circumcision; while
the time from Moses forward is characterized by the fully
developed Mosaic system. It would seem that the Priestly
school gave the final shaping to the material in Genesis and,
again, that it sought to stress theological themes rather than
simply provide a step-by-step account of what had taken place.

1. The Creation Story (1-3)

Although chapters 1 and 2 specifically speak of creation,
the first three chapters must be considered together. The
purposes of chapters 1 and 2 can be seen only with the culmination of the message in chapter 3.

God's Sovereign Purpose for Man (1-2)

It might be well to note that other creation stories have
been found with such similarities as to suggest either that the
framework is borrowed from the framework of the contemporary world or vice versa or that both have borrowed and
adapted from a common source. Should it be discovered that
the Bible writers have done the adapting, there would be no
cause for alarm. After all, here might be the genius of biblical
inspiration and revelation—the taking of the generally accepted concept of the world which was prevalent in the
writer's day, the same concept which has been passed on from
Mesopotamian times, and using the story as a vehicle, a parable, or a framework for showing the proper and revealed
concept of God.

There are numerous creation stories of other cultures of
earlier literary form but with similar cosmological views.
Only the more significant of these need be noticed. "Creation
by Atum" is a text which was carved inside the pyramid of

Mer-ne-Re and Pepi II, about the twenty-fourth century B.C.[1]
According to the legend, Atum was the creator God who
sneezed (cf. the J account, Gen. 2:7, of God breathing life
into man) and through the sneeze formed Shu, god of the air,
and Tefnut, goddess of moisture. Parallel to this, the KA of
Atum, i.e., the guardian spirit of the vital force of personality,
was placed in the first creatures.

One is reminded here of the *ruach* (life substance) of Genesis. Additional beings followed, and each of the other creatures was charged with some portion of the universe: Geb,
god of earth; Nut, goddess of the sky; Osiris, god of the underworld; and several others, who all received their life from the
supreme god. The legend emphasizes the sovereignty and
creatorship of a divine being. Superior to the legend, the
book of Genesis gives a much clearer and more sensible
picture and identification relative to the divine being and how
he works, even though there are a few parts of the literary
vehicle with vague similarities.

In a second version of "Creation by Atum," to be dated
about 2000 B.C.,[2] life is pictured as rising forth from watery
chaos (Nun). This is a similar note to that of the "*ruach* of
God hovering over the face of the waters" in Genesis 1:2. The
god who causes the life to rise forth from the watery chaos is
represented as saying, "I am yesterday, while I know tomor-
row." It is a claim to be the God of time and eternity. Is
not this the attribute of the *true* God of Genesis 1?

Better known than either version of the above story is the
Babylonian creation story, usually known as *Enuma Elish*.
This work consisted of seven tablets and was named from the
first words of tablet 1, *Enuma Elish*, or "When on High." The
tablets were perhaps recited each New Year on the fourth day
of the New Year festival as a part of creativity and fertility

---

[1]James B. Pritchard (ed.), *Ancient Near Eastern Texts* (Princeton: Princeton
University Press, 1955), p. 3.
[2]*Ibid.*

rites. Those texts available go back to about 1000 B.C. (almost a thousand years older than any of the available texts of the Old Testament), but there is evidence that the written source actually goes back to an original composition of 2000 B.C.

A brief summary of the story for comparative purposes will have to suffice. Basically, it is a story dealing with the struggle between chaos and cosmic order. Originally existent were two monstrous dragons known as Apsu, the fresh-water subterranean ocean, and his consort, Tiamat, the salt-water ocean that surrounded the earth. (*Tiamat* apparently has etymological kinship with *Tehom,* the Hebrew word for "deep" in the Genesis narrative).

From this original pair sprang various generations of deities until finally some of the younger ones garnered great power. There ensued a battle of the gods in which one Ea slew Apsu while his son Marduk (the god Bel of Babylon) waged a dreadful battle and slew Tiamat. The great wind blew into Tiamat's body; thence, Marduk took his sword and sliced Tiamat in the middle. Heaven was made with the top of her, and with her lower half the earth was made.

Finally, mankind was created from the blood of Kingu, Tiamat's chief minister. After such a superior display, Marduk was elevated to the position of supreme god, whereby all other gods conferred their power upon him. The making of man from Kingu's blood may suggest that there is a touch of the divine in man or that in some way man is in the god's image. As is well known by now, there are many similarities between *Enuma Elish* and Genesis. In both stories, seven stages are present in the creative process. Note the similarities in sequence of events:

Enuma Elish	*Genesis 1 to 2:*4a
1. Divine spirit and cosmic matter are coexistent and co-eternal.	1. Divine spirit exists independent of cosmic matter.

2. Primeval chaos, Tiamat enveloped in darkness.

3. Light emanating from the gods.

4. Creation of the firmament.

5. Creation of the dry land.

6. Creation of the luminaries.

7. Creation of man.

8. Gods rest and celebrate (man was to serve from here on).

2. Earth a desolate waste with darkness covering the deep.

3. Light created.

4. Creation of the firmament.

5. Creation of the dry land.

6. Creation of the luminaries.

7. Creation of man.

8. The Lord rests and sanctifies the seventh day.

This identical sequence of events is remarkable when the fact is considered that this particular sequence was not necessary from the standpoint of logic. But it is in the dissimilarities that comparison is important. The book of Genesis always takes for granted only one divine principle, independent of all cosmic matter, while the Babylonian story assumes the existence of two sexually different divine beings from whose union all else was descended. But the telling blow is that the Genesis story is monotheistic, while *Enuma Elish* is polytheistic. In Genesis the Creator clearly is the one living God.

Perhaps one of the basic purposes for which the book of Genesis was written was to correct the false impression of deity held by many of the world's people. From the beginning the book must have been designed to have this universal mission and purpose.

Another striking similarity which is to be inferred from Genesis is the world view assumed. "Inferred" is the proper word, for Genesis alone gives insufficient details for completing the picture. However, other sections of the Bible furnish additional information. The concept implied—one which the Babylonians seemed to hold also—was something like that which follows below:[3]

---

[3] Cf. S. H. Hooke, "In the Beginning," *The Clarendon Bible* (Oxford: Clarendon Press, 1947), p. 20.

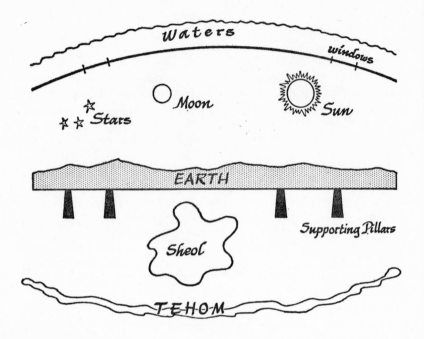

The Firmament—Genesis 1:6-8, apparently indicated a solid mass, for the word means "something beat out."

Luminaries—Genesis 1:14-19.

Pillars—Job 9:8; 26:5-14.

The Waters—Genesis 1:7; 7:11; Psalm 104:3; 148:4; 78:23; Job 38: 22; 2 Kings 7:2; Genesis 8:2.

The Deep—Psalm 139:9.

The Underworld (Sheol)—Jonah 2:7; Psalm 61:3; Genesis 37: 35; 42:38; 44:29-31; Numbers 16:30,38.

This is the setting of the stage on which the drama is to unfold. The compiler used the concept of the world prevalent in his day as a vehicle for showing the proper concept of God! Here is another evidence of the "baptism" of a concept for theological purposes.

Is there nothing distinctive which Genesis on its own presents? Very definitely and uniquely there is. Creation originated in the will of God (1:3 f). God's speech—"Let there be light," etc.,—is always prior to, and makes possible, the existence of something. Thus, everything "owes its existence to God's creative word"; hence, it is all good. This step-by-step design suggests that God works with a pattern and purpose. There is nothing here of the irrational or whimsical. All is according to the willed design of God. Hence, God is a personal being. He transcends the universe and is independent of the universe. There is not the slightest room for pantheism here.

Moreover, as Köhler has suggested:

Creation in Old Testament theology is an eschatological concept. The fact that God is the creator of the world means that He compasses the complete time process, ruling, determining, and completing all ages. That is why He is called the first and the last, (Isa. 44:6).[4]

To speak of "a personal God who wills creation" means that he is absolute sovereign over what he has created. This is important to notice, for it lays down a fundamental principle and background for what is to follow; i.e., that God is sovereign over created society and human life; and if man fails to recognize this, he sins and gets into trouble. Furthermore, it underscores the truth that the history of God's people gets its meaning through creation.[5]

Thus, the first two chapters place emphasis on what God did and thereby enunciate monotheism in its highest expression. The strength of the principle can more easily be seen if one will take a pencil and circle the word "God" (Elohim) each time it occurs in chapters 1 and 2. Elohim, probably from a

---

[4]Ludwig Köhler, *Old Testament Theology,* trans. A. S. Todd (Philadelphia: Westminster Press, 1953), p. 88.

[5]*Ibid.,* p. 87.

root meaning "strength" or "power," occurs forty-six times in these two chapters. It is demonstrably clear that the message is GOD, with the parallels of man's dependence upon him and relationship to him, with the intricacies of detail assuming a place of less importance. God *before* all, God *back* of all, God *above* all are appropriate statements.[6]

The First or Priestly Account of Creation (1:1 to 2:4a)

1:1-2. The very first phrase of the Bible has been the object of much discussion among scholars across the years. Cognizance of this debate was taken by the Revised Standard Version translators, for in the body appears, "In the beginning God created the heavens and the earth," while the footnote reads, "When God began to create. . . ."

Perhaps the crux is whether the verse does or does not speak of absolute creation. Rashi and Ibn Ezra, leading rabbinical commentators on the Bible, approached the first clause as a temporal one, subordinate to either both or one of the first two verses, and read it as follows, "In the beginning of God's creating the heavens and the earth." With such a translation, *b^ereshith* would be construct state followed by a clause used as genitive.[7] The Brown, Driver, and Briggs *Lexicon* gives *reshith* as a feminine substantive and lists it as signifying the best or first part of a thing.[8]

Consequently, the phrase would not signify creation in the absolute sense of the creation of material substance; it would simply denote the first stage of a process or series of events, corresponding to a Hebrew usage which is to be found in Hosea 9:10; Deuteronomy 11:12; Job 8:7; 40:19; and Isaiah 46:10. Possible support here is the failure to use a definite article with the word "beginning" (there is none in the He-

---

[6]Sampey, *op. cit.*, p. 13.

[7]Skinner, *op. cit.*, p. 12.

[8]Francis Brown, S. R. Driver, and Charles A. Briggs, *A Hebrew and English Lexicon of the Old Testament* (Oxford: Clarendon Press, 1952), p. 912.

brew, although most English translations supply one), which would have aided an absolute understanding. But a major objection—one which cannot be lightly considered—is the vowel pointing of the verb *bara'*. If a construct meaning is intended, the verb ought to be pointed as an infinitive or as a participle and not as a *qal* perfect, as all texts point it.

Walter Eichrodt probably is correct in championing the sense of absolute creation.[9] This has to do with the absolute beginning of things—something which cannot be repeated. God did that which man cannot do; therefore, man is dependent upon him and must recognize him.[10] Thus, verses 1 and 2 seem to be an introductory heading to the remainder of the chapter. Intended in chapter 1 is a narration of the whole creative process. After the general summation in these verses, the remaining verses outline the steps. The completed picture is first presented. Then are announced the details which lead to the completion. Various words and combinations of words must be treated for the clarification of the entire presentation.[11]

In beginning is out of regular Hebrew order, standing first in the sentence when normally it would come at the end. This must be for the purpose of emphasizing the absolute fact of creation, that nothing existed before God. The word *bara'* (created) continues the emphasis, for it is a word used exclusively of divine activity.[12] It is doubtful that such a restriction can be found in any other language. Generally, the idea of an extraordinary or unusual result is implied (cf. Isa. 48:6 f.; 41:20; 65:17 f.; Jer. 31:21; Ex. 34:10; Num. 16:30), and the work done seems to be effortless, such as would befit the will

---

[9]Walter Eichrodt, *Theologie des Alten Testaments* (Berlin: Evangelische Verlagsastalt, 1950), II, 507 f.

[10]Dietrich Bonhoeffer, *Creation and Fall*, trans. John C. Fletcher (New York: Macmillan Co., 1959), pp. 9-17.

[11]Words and phrases will be discussed from time to time in the order and construction in which they occur in the Hebrew Bible and not as they appear in translation. This assures comprehension of the intended emphasis.

[12]George A. F. Knight, *A Christian Theology of the Old Testament* (Richmond: John Knox Press, 1959), p. 110.

or desire of God (cf. Psalm 33:9).[13]   Although the first in-disputable claim for creation out of nothing (*creatio ex nihilo*) does not appear in Jewish literature until 2 Maccabees 7:28, such seems to be taken for granted in the Genesis passage. At any rate, the interpreter so understood it in Hebrews 11:3.

The all inclusive nature of God's creation is indicated in the phrase "the heavens and the earth."   Heaven signified the dwelling place of God, while earth was man's dwelling.   The author is suggesting that all below, above, and in between is the handiwork of God.

"Without form and void," or "waste and void" as *thohu wavohu* is sometimes translated, is the description given in the second verse.   In 1791, Dathe, followed by Chalmers, championed by Harry Rimmer, and adopted by the Scofield Bible, used this verse as the basis of the so-called gap theory of creation.   He adopted a suggestion of three stages—sometimes called original creation, judgment and ruination, and re-creation.   Supposedly, God created a perfect world (1:1, "original creation"); but this perfect world was ruined by the fall of Lucifer and was left waste for millions of years—time enough for the geological formations to take place.   Ezekiel 28 is cited as a proof text.   Re-creation followed, when in 4004 B.C. God reconditioned the earth in six literal twenty-four-hour periods.   The specific date was adopted from James Ussher (1581-1656), an Irish bishop, who calculated the year, while Lightfoot, a Hebrew scholar from Cambridge, meticu-lously calculated the time as October 23 at 9 A.M., 45th me-ridian.   To support such a theory, the verb *hayah* of 1:2, the verb "to be," is translated as "became" rather than "was."

The frequent misconception of "chaos" and the gap theory would be avoided if the more accurate translation of "formless-ness and emptiness" were used—formlessness and emptiness in the sense of not yet having life and order.

---

[13]Skinner, *op. cit.*, p. 15.

To believe that Lucifer could destroy God's perfect creation is to make Lucifer stronger than God. The attestation of verse 2 is the exact opposite, for it is stated that "the spirit of God was hovering over the face of the waters." God was intimately concerned with, and related to, his creation. To follow such a theory is to make the first chapter of the Bible speak about reconstruction and not creation. It is illogical that just two sentences would be devoted to original creation with nothing in the prologomena of God's plan for man definitely connecting God with a strong claim on original creation.

Hayethah is definitely a perfect, indicative of the completed state "was" and not "becoming" or "became." One suspects that the theory arose in an effort to harmonize the geological ages of science with the seven days of creation. Such a theory does not solve the problems, however, for geology sees the gradual emergence of better life and not the going of the good to the chaotic.

As suggested by Alleman and Flack, the passage simply speaks of the earth as "an empty and undeveloped state."[14] The earth here seems to be a watery mass in which the future elements of land and sea are contained. In other words, here one is told that God made the clay. In verses 3 ff., that clay is viewed as it is shaped into various aspects. This helps in understanding the purpose which seems to be implied in the Hebrew construction of Isaiah 45:18, "for the purpose of form-lessness he did not create it; for the purpose of dwelling he fashioned it." An imperfect but simple parallel from modern industry might help. A concern may manufacture plastic. Then from the plastic which has already been manufactured, toys of different shapes and sizes are molded. God created the world in elemental form and from it brought forth the ordered existence known to us. Verses 1 and 2 relate that he created the material; verses 3 ff. delineate what he "manufactured"

---

[14]Herbert C. Alleman and Elmer E. Flack, *Old Testament Commentary* (Philadelphia: Muhlenberg Press, 1948), p. 173.

out of that material. Perhaps this is why the term *asah,* to make out of already existent materials, is used elsewhere in the chapter.

The word translated "spirit" in verse 2 is really the word for breath or power. Tracing a similar usage in *Enuma Elish,* the Septuagint, and in the Targum of Onkelos, Orlinsky translates *ruach* as "strong force."[15] It indicates the presence of God, the eternal and infinite Spirit, Creator and Sovereign of the universe. God was there; he knew what he was doing and controlled what was happening.

1:3-25. Although the modern mind would say that there could be no light without sun, moon, and stars (not created until the fourth day), the first thing pictured in God's creation was light. In the mind of the Priestly writer, the elements of light and darkness, air and matter were all part of basic material which could be called forth as God desired. Various interpretations have been offered in an effort to explain the meaning of "light."

Some of the rabbis suggested that this was a special light which was operative only during the seven days of creation.[16] Others liked the "appearance theory," which suggests that the stars were created in the beginning but did not make their appearance until four days later. God's work was thought to be that of the clearing and purification of the atmosphere so that the rays from the light bodies could break through. Delitzsch tried to be more scientific in his interpretation when he suggested that the first thing created was "light material," to be distinguished from the "lights" or "light bearers," which were created on the fourth day. According to Delitzsch, it is "now a generally accepted truth of natural science, that the light does not spring from the sun and stars, but that the sun

---

[15]Harry M. Orlinsky, "The Plain Meaning of Ruªh in Gen. 1:2," *The Jewish Quarterly Review,* XLVIII (October, 1957), 174-182.

[16]A. Cohen (ed.), *The Soncino Chumash* (London: Soncino Press, 1947), p. 1.

itself is a dark body, and the light proceeds from an atmosphere which surrounds it."[17]

Scientific explanation is impossible, and the attempt is an erroneous approach to interpretation. Here again is the carry-over of the literary vehicle from its Babylonian counterpart. According to the Babylonians, Marduk the creator was a solar deity; his appearance is often interpreted as the appearance of light at the beginning of creation. Probably in the Genesis account also, light is thought of as a thing in itself and independent of the heavenly light bodies (cf. Job 38:19-20). As someone has suggested:

This is really not a true problem. The Hebrews had often noticed that despite the absence of the sun (as for example on dark and gloomy days) there was light. And as every morning light preceded the rising of the sun, they concluded that light was in some way independent of the sun. What precisely was their scientific idea? Who can say? When at the beginning of the second three-days, the sun was commanded to "rule the day," its role was perhaps thought to consist in emphasizing by its presence the separation of the day from the night, and to act as a sign for the establishing of the calendar. The sun was to illuminate the earth; it was not, however, to be the sole and exclusive source of light.[18]

Since in the Babylonian story there had to be a separation of light from chaotic darkness, the writer here is borrowing and adapting from literature to show that God had such complete control of things he could separate light and darkness, could bring good out of that which was chaotic. This again emphasizes God's sovereignty. When the luminaries are introduced on the fourth day, another note of sovereignty is sounded. Whereas the rest of the ancient world thought that

---

[17]C. F. Keil and F. Delitzsch, *The Pentateuch*, Vol. I: *Biblical Commentary on the Old Testament*, trans. James Martin (Grand Rapids: Wm. B. Eerdman's Publishing Co., 1951), p. 49.

[18]Charles Hauret, *Beginnings: Genesis and Modern Science*, trans. E. P. Emmans (Dubuque: Priory Press, 1955), p. 53.

the heavenly bodies were animated, in some way divine or to be identified as gods (cf. Isa. 40:26; Job 38:7; Judg. 5:20), such is denied in Genesis. God was not *in* the luminaries; he created them.

Since the discussion of light and day is inevitable, perhaps it would be well to introduce here a consideration of the days of creation and some suggestions as to the meaning of "day."

It is interesting to note that in the delineation of the days, evening is mentioned first. At least as early as the fourth century B.C.,[19] and perhaps earlier, the Hebrews reckoned a day from "sunset to sunset." Such usage here may indicate that the Hebrew writer was imposing his concept of time on the story. But what is to be understood by these seven periods called days? Superficially, the most plausible explanation is that of a twenty-four-hour period. However, to accept such amounts to a disregard of what science has to say about the age of the earth. Such tests as the salinity of the ocean, the age of the rocks, and the chemical analysis of material remains point to an earth two to four billion years old.

Augustine approached the problem from an entirely different standpoint, although still accepting the day as a twenty-four-hour period. According to Augustine, during these twenty-four-hour periods, "seminal principles" were sown in nature. During the seven days, the living things which inhabit the earth were created potentially in the form of "hidden seed," or "seminal causes." In due time these "hidden seed," or "seminal causes," sprouted forth and grew according to God's own good time and pleasure.[20] This would allow for some evolution. Indeed, Thomas Aquinas (1225-1274), Italian monk and theologian, felt that evolution was the *modus operandi* by which the "hidden seed" became actualities.[21]

---

[19]T. C. Smith, *Jesus in the Gospel of John* (Nashville: Broadman Press, 1959), p. 8.

[20]W. A. Christian, "Augustine on the Creation of the World," *Harvard Theological Review,* XLVI (Jan., 1953), 1-25.

[21]*Ibid.*

Contrasted with the twenty-four-hour period is what at times is called the "divine day," a suggestion that the periods were not necessarily of the same length. Whatever time was necessary for the various processes and developments transpired. Later, on the basis of this pattern of seven creative periods, the human week of seven days was used.[22] Some "period of time" similar to the "divine day" must be the answer. Although it is not authority for either the acceptance or rejection of the view, it is accepted by many geologists, even though the phrase used is often "geologic day."

Quite often in the Scriptures the term used here, *yom,* commonly translated as "day," unequivocably indicates a period of time and not a twenty-four-hour day. This is true in all three sections of the canon.[23] In this immediate context, Genesis 2:4, *yom* is used to refer to the entire period of creation. Reinforcing its acceptance is the fact that the sun and heavenly bodies, which determine our twenty-four-hour day, were not created until the fourth day. Thus, at least the first *three* days were not twenty-four-hour days as modern man knows them, for the sun's rising and not its setting determines our day. This is to say little of the produce of the earth. The grass, herbs, and trees yielded seed and bore fruit. Such does not happen in a twenty-four-hour period.

It is to be concluded then that these are periods of indefinite length. One cannot, however, identify these indefinite periods with the geological ages as laid down in the textbooks of geology. Not all geologists agree in identification nor can it be maintained definitely that every geological age covered the entire surface of the earth.[24] This is in keeping with the pattern in Genesis itself, where the day of rest seems to encompass time from the creation of man to the present.

---

[22]*Ibid.*

[23]Cf. Isa. 2:11; Jer. 39:16; Ezek. 29:21; Gen. 30:14; Num. 13:20; Deut. 24:15; Josh. 3:15; and Prov. 25:13.

[24]Albertus Pieters, *Notes on Genesis* (Grand Rapids: Wm. B. Eerdman's Publishing Co., 1954), I, 33.

1:26 to 2:4a. As the creation of man is approached, several distinct differences are to be noted. Instead of the jussive third person, the cohortative first person, "let us," is used. Man was initiated by a solemn announcement rather than by a command. The lower animals were made each after their kind, but man was made after the *image of God*. Appointed as head of all other creation (1:26), man was the pearl, the crown of creation.

About the other creation God said that "it was good" but of man he said "very good" (1:31), indicating something of the high value placed on mankind. This is to be seen also in the "image of God" expression. The two words here are "image" and "likeness." Linguistically, the word "image" implies a hewn or carved statue or a "copy" of something else while "likeness" similarly means a facsimile. Thus, the words do not imply that man is divine. He is copied after a divine one, patterned after a divine one with some of his attributes; he has functions which are like God's. Thus, God showed himself to be the *prototype* and the *original* of man. This implies, not that man is just like God, but that man is something on the order of God. He is to represent the sovereignty and the royal prerogatives of God in this world.

Characteristically, biblical tradition and Judaism have been opposed to anything that would suggest physical likeness to God. This is fundamental in the ten basic principles of religion found in Exodus 20. The very terms "image" and "likeness" denote the absolute difference between God and man.[25] Thus, the similarity here is to be found in an area other than physical. It is more of a "moral likeness" in which man as a morally responsible individual is capable, because of fellowship with God, of having dominion over the remainder of God's creation. From the standpoint of theology, this implies not only fellowship but also representation.

---

[25]Th. C. Vriezen, *An Outline of Old Testament Theology* (Oxford: Basil Blackwell & Mott, Ltd., 1958), p. 145.

Images in the Orient were to represent someone. Thus, man is the "representative" of God over creation.[26] Actually, the image idea has something to say about man's stewardship. Dependence is also involved; man is dependent upon the one for whom he is representative.[27] Since dependent man has been delegated a task of responsibility with a share of authority over creation, he is in turn a responsible being.

In passing, it is important to note that the image of God in man is present both before and after the Fall (Gen. 1:26 f.; 5:1,3; 9:6). Neither the Fall nor the Flood destroyed it. This is a basic trait which God has stamped upon all mankind. Man may ignore this character, act on the animal level, and, thus in a sense, be "inhuman" in the nature of failing to evaluate and use the possibilities which God has graciously given; but he does not *lose* these possibilities. As long as there is life, there is the opportunity through forgiveness of having dominion and fellowship with God.

The expression "let *us* make man" presents questions which are impossible to answer to everyone's satisfaction. Some form of it is used several other times (Gen. 3:22; 11:7; Isa. 6:8), and the phrase is variously interpreted.

Christian commentators, including Calvin, for a long time have suggested that here is to be found the Trinity in the Old Testament. But nowhere is there any evidence that such a doctrine was known by the people whom God used to give birth to the Old Testament.

Such a concept could be understood only after the coming of the Son. If such a doctrine had been held, it would have paved the way for the Jews for an easier acceptance of the Messiah. As it was, they thought it quite presumptuous that anyone should dare claim such a thing as sonship (cf. Matt. 26:63).

---

[26]Edmond Jacob, *Theology of the Old Testament,* trans. Arthur W. Heathcote and Philip J. Allcock (London: Hodder & Stoughton, Ltd., 1958), p. 167.
[27]*Ibid.,* p. 171.

Of necessity, a doctrine of sonship would have involved the doctrine of the Holy Spirit, and at no point in the Old Testament is personality given to the Spirit. The only passages which come close are Psalm 51:11 and Isaiah 63:11, and in both instances "holy" is simply a descriptive word—"spirit of thy holiness" and "spirit of his holiness." Of course, this is not to say that there *was* no Trinity until New Testament times. Even though man's understanding may have been delayed, God's nature has always been the same.

That the plural "let us" is a remnant of polytheism is even more unacceptable. To be sure, older literature may have furnished a literary framework for the Genesis account, but it must not be forgotten that into this was to be poured a distinctive theology. Never, especially in the strongly monotheistic Priestly source, would such a false characterization of the true God be allowed to remain.

More favor can be directed to the "God and the hosts of heaven" interpretation; i.e., that the "us" includes the angels, seraphim, and others in the court of heaven (cf. Isa. 6; Job 1; 1 Kings 22:19; Deut. 33; Ex. 15:11). Thus, God may be taking counsel with, or addressing, the angels. However, since the Priestly source has as part of its purpose emphasis upon genuine monotheism, such an interpretation, which gives the heavenly beings some share in creation, would be contradictory. This also is contrary to biblical teaching elsewhere. God's angels always appear as servants and never as an advisory council.

A variation of this approach is the suggestion that God is projecting his thoughts or "blueprint" ahead and that the "us" refers to Adam and Eve, who will have the privilege of participating with God in creation.[28] But this is no solution; for it attempts to answer a question by creating a similar one—

---

[28]The author was first exposed to this variation in conversations with J. J. Owens at the Southern Baptist Theological Seminary, in Louisville, Kentucky, but he has not found it in literary form.

from whence or by what means came Adam and Eve. In this suggestion, nothing is said about their creation.

There remains only one interpretation of merit. It is what is commonly called "plural of majesty." Reigning monarchs often think of themselves as "we." When the monarch speaks of "we," he has in mind his power, majesty, lordship, splendor, honor, and other characteristics or attributes which may be his in the eyes of his subjects. Skinner objects that this usage is not found elsewhere in Hebrew theology.[29]

However, three usages are sufficient to show that, though not customary usage, this method was coined to show the peculiar nature of God.[30] This is especially acceptable since the usage occurs in two of the documents, P (Gen. 1:26) and J (Gen. 3:22; 11:7), and in Isaiah, the one prophetic book which stresses most the holiness of God. Involved here is a synthesis of the fulness of the powers of God in creation—a "plural of majesty."

So much attention has been directed to "let us" that often "man" is overlooked. Startling though it may be, it is imperative to note that the word for mankind in a collective sense ('adam) is used and not man in the sense of one individual man ('ish). If one individual man were intended here, it is strange that the word meaning specifically an individual was passed by for a word that generally has a wider reference. In the 510 times that 'adam occurs, it seldom, with any certainty, means an individual man rather than man in a collective sense.[31]

In Genesis 1:26 it is very evident in the use of the plural pronoun, "let *them*," that woman is also included in the term, for this is to be seen in the command, "Be fruitful and multiply and replenish the earth and subdue it." By analogy with the land and marine animals, the context argues *against* the crea-

---

[29]Skinner, *op. cit.*, p. 30.
[30]S. R. Driver, *The Book of Genesis* (London: Methuen & Co., Ltd., 1911), p. 14.
[31]Köhler, *op. cit.*, p. 129.

tion of a single man and a single woman. Nothing in the context suggests a change from the collective creation of pairs of animals to a single pair of humans.

Elsewhere in the Old Testament there are no *clear* references to *'adam* as one man. Hosea 6:7 is often translated, "But like Adam they transgressed." There is nothing in this passage to show, however, that reference to a specific individual is intended. "But like mankind" is equally correct. Job 31:33 reads, "If I have concealed my transgressions from *'adam.*" This is variously translated as "Adam" or "men." It is evident that Job is speaking of "men" collectively and not "Adam" singularly.

It would appear more probable that the Genesis passage is speaking of the creation of the human race even as it speaks of the creation of various classes of animal and vegetable life. There is certainly the possibility that God created more than one man and that he subsequently used one pair, Adam and Eve, to typify what happened to all men. Even as Adam and Eve sinned, so it was characteristic that all mankind sinned. Very definitely, chapter 3 takes one pair as an example. If this be the case, it alleviates such questions as "where did Cain get his wife?" There were others whom God had created and from whom Cain could choose.

Another insight is presented by the Priestly writer. Woman is not created *after* man but *along* with him. Thus, men and women are of equal importance and are to complement each other. God did not intend man to be superior in original creation, even as in the new creation there is to be no distinction (cf. Gal. 3:28).[32]

Following the creation of man, God brought forth the seventh day; and according to 2:2, it was on the seventh day that God finished the work which he had done. The verse indicates that God concluded the finishing touches on the seventh day and rested. The picture of God's laboring on the

---

[32]Richardson, *op. cit.*, p. 56.

seventh day affords problems. The Septuagint, the Syriac, and the Samaritan Pentateuch all read, "on the *sixth* day God finished. . . ." Possibly a scribal error was made in the manuscript on which the Masoretic text is based. On the other hand, if the present text is correct, it may indicate that God *surveyed* the situation on the sabbath and decided that he would do no more. Thus, from then on, the sabbath was a rest day.

"Finish" does not mean "to turn things loose." God finished the basic creative activity, but his work still goes on. This might have some bearing on the "divine day" theory, in which the seventh day indicates that God finished the initial creative activity and now is engaged in labors of another type.

At any rate, God blessed the seventh day and sanctified it. It was set apart from the ordinary and common things and put to holy uses with a special relation to God. Apparently, the Hebrews believed that it was endowed with permanently beneficial qualities (cf. Gen. 27:27; Ex. 23:25; Deut. 28:12). Thus, the P record closes with a picture of peace, rest, harmony, and blessing—God's desire for man and the universe which he had made.

The Second Creation Account (2:4b-25)

2:4b-6. This is the J account which is included, not because the writer or editor failed to harmonize, but in order to present other theological implications of the fact of creation. Chapter 1, or the Priestly account, emphasizes that God did it, primarily showing the *power* behind creation and the *monotheistic nature* of that power. The emphasis of chapter 2 is that though God is *Lord* over it, his creation was to be a *fellowship* between him and man.

Some differences are to be noted in the emphases and details of the two stories. Although man follows plant life in the first account and is the last and climactic act of creation, in the second account he precedes the plant life. The Priestly source deals with the total heavenly host, while the Yahweh source is concerned only with the setting in a local garden. Man and woman were formed by the same creative act in the first account, but in the second source two separate processes are involved. A watery mass is replaced with the dry plain in chapter 2. It is evident that neither account is trying to give an accurate point-by-point description outlining the order of creation but that these are vehicles for conveying spiritual truth. The present account emphasizes man as a spiritual being.

2:7. The phrase, "God formed . . . and breathed" is perhaps the J account's equivalent to the "image of God" in the P source. It is not said that God breathed his breath into the animals. Perhaps it should be said, then, that man lives by the breath of God, that he has a nature or a spark in him which makes him kin to, or patterned after, the divine, even though he is not divine. This deduction is to be made from "God breathed" and not from the phrase "became a living soul" (being).

The phrase *nephesh hayah* (living being) is used both of human life (2:7) and animal life (2:19), but this is obscured in most English translations. Wishing, perhaps, to avoid the ascription of human characteristics to animal life, the King James translators used "living soul" in 2:7 and "living creature" in 2:19. The Revised Standard Version has "living being" and "living creature." It is better to translate *nephesh hayah* as "living being" and not "living soul," for an animal does not have a soul. Verse 7 thus means that man *is* a living being; it is not concerned with the concept that man *has* a living being (soul). *Nephesh* is what results when the *basar* (flesh) is animated by *ruach* (spirit, wind, life). Although the Greeks divided man into the three parts of body, mind, and soul, this was not true among the Hebrews. To them, a man's body was but the outward expression of his inner being; they thought of man as an animated body. God was interested in the redemption of the total being, not merely in a single part of man called a "soul." Perhaps a more mature concept of salvation could be gathered today if New Testament exegetes would fathom more carefully the Hebraic background from which the New Testament thought came.

As the phrase "God breathed" is used here, it simply says that man, like the animals, also became a living being (creature). This has nothing to do with the part of man which responds to God. It is the fact that *God breathed* which makes man different from the animals. In this sense, man is like God—God's breath is in him. Because he has a body, he is like the animals. Consequently, man enjoys the privileges of participating in a good world with the capabilities of growth and fellowship with God.

2:8-17. Needless to say, the Garden of Eden cannot be located. The river mentioned in Genesis and in the midst of the garden is supposed to have branched out into four rivers— the Pishon, Gihon, Hiddekel (Tigris, cf. Dan. 10:4 and the writings of Strabo and Pliny), and the Euphrates. Because today the Tigris and the Euphrates have different sources, it is fruitless to try to find from the Genesis description an exact location.

Since so much of ancient literature has a setting in paradise, it would seem that the biblical story does not intend to indicate an actual place but rather to suggest a setting for the message to be conveyed. "Garden" (*'eden*) can be translated as "garden of delight" or "paradise." Thus, the purpose of the story is to indicate that man was created by God to dwell in the happiness of a paradisiacal existence, that is, in fellowship with God and in the enjoyment of all that God had made.

The tree of life also is not an unusual feature for ancient literature. Outside the Bible, however, it is represented as standing in a place quite inaccesible to man. In the Genesis record the tree of life is in the part of the garden in which man is to dwell. Thus, God originally intended that man should enjoy his blessing. God intended that he should eat of the tree of life, which is representative of the blessing of God. The idyllic setting is representative of man's unbroken communion with God. It was this kind of fellowship that man broke by his sin.

Thus, in troubled times, the prophet Ezekiel (47:12) looked forward to a better day as symbolized by life-giving trees in the new Jerusalem. There are similar, more specific references in Revelation 2:7 and 22:14. The fact that the symbol was later used in these ways is evidence of its original intention. God had wanted man to have life, but it was to be secured in a worthy manner. However, God knew that after man disobeyed and ate of the tree of knowledge he would realize that he would die, and he would want the tree of life. Thus, in 3:24, the tree of life had to be guarded lest man try to take of it before being purified. Notice that originally it was of the tree of knowledge of good and evil that God forbade him eat, not the tree of life.

With reference to the tree of knowledge of good and evil, the Hebrew terms *ra'* (evil) and *tov* (good) do not signify, primarily, moral good and evil. Their fundamental meaning is good and evil as they bear on the physical well-being of man, i.e., helpful and harmful.

George Buchanan[33] has made a good case for linking this with the mature knowledge which God gives man through experience and blessing. A survey of use in other passages would indicate that maturity, possibly twenty years of age, is never ruled out as a possible interpretation. Twenty years of age is suggested, for twenty years and upward was the age at which inclusion for military service was made (cf. Num. 1:2,20,22,24,28,30, etc.; 26:2; 32:11; 1 Chron. 27:23; 2 Chron. 25:6). It was the age at which tax was to be paid (Lev. 27:3).

---

[33]George Wesley Buchanan, "The Old Testament Meaning of the Knowledge of Good and Evil," *Journal of Biblical Literature*, LXXV (June, 1956), 114-120.

Those who were ruled out of entrance into the land of Canaan were twenty or more years of age, old enough to have known better than to sin (Num. 14:29-30).

The parallel to this is Deuteronomy 1:39, where the terms *ra'* and *tov* are actually used. This verse says that the land will be given only to those who have no knowledge of good and evil, i.e., are not yet twenty years of age. In Isaiah 7:14-17, desolation was forecast prior to a certain child's attainment of an age when he could refuse the evil and choose the good. If this meant before the child became twenty, then the fall of Samaria (722 B.C.) was well within the twenty-year period commencing with the 735 B.C. prediction. Barzillai complained in 2 Samuel 19:35 that he was eighty years of age and could not discern what was good. Apparently, he meant that he lacked the good judgment and ideal keenness which he had when he was only twenty years old.[34]

But even with such a preponderance of evidence, the case is not definitely concluded. Often sexual consciousness has been connected with the tree of knowledge. The suggestion has been made that perhaps the proper solution is in combining both elements. To have mature knowledge involves knowing how to reproduce, which has some similarity to God's ability to create. Man's sin in part involved producing and creating without thinking that God had anything to do with it. One would have to conclude, however, that although this is *part* of the mature knowledge which comes through experience, it is certainly not the whole. All knowledge—human experience in its totality—is included. The point is that man should not try to get this knowledge for and by himself. This is a mature knowledge which is the prerequisite of God and which can be properly attained only through God-guided experiences.

To act as though one already has the knowledge which only God can give is to grasp a function which properly belongs to God. Basically, the sin involved is pride, trying to be *as*

---

[34]*Ibid.*, p. 118.

God. Man too often feigns or desires omniscience, thus putting himself at the center of the stage rather than God. God wanted man to have life (tree of life), but it was to be obtained only as God granted the experiences (tree of knowledge) validating life.

2:18-25. The creation of woman was to fulfil a desire to give man a "helpmeet," "a helper to meet him face to face ['ezer]." As Richardson suggests, this does not indicate a kind of "first mate with man as the skipper"[35] but one equally responsible. A good translation is "a helper answering to him"— one who "answers," one with whom the self can enter into responsible relations. Dr. Sampey suggested this when he said ". . . not made out of his head to rule over him; nor out of his feet to be trampled on by him; but out of his side, to be equal with him; under his arm to be protected; and near his heart to be beloved."[36]

Man and woman, *'ish* and *'ishah*—there was an original equality but a difference in function (2:22). Adam expressed great pleasure with woman. She was to be his first, last, and always. After he had looked at all of the animals and not found satisfaction, he found satisfaction in woman. This was part of God's blessing in creation. The perpetuation of this part of the blessing was to be assured through monogamy (2:24). At times in the Old Testament polygamy is apparently permissive; but the right state, as indicated here, is for each man to cleave unto his wife. Jesus interprets it so in Matthew 19:5 and Mark 10:7.

This extended treatment has been an effort to show something of the basic theological purpose in the first two chapters. Perhaps it now can be understood that the creation stories are not scientific treatises about the world. They are to help man understand the basic nature of his relationship to God. Thus, there is no cause for alarm when Dr. George K. Schweitzer,

---

[35]Richardson, *op. cit.*, p. 66.
[36]Sampey, *op. cit.*, pp. 19-20.

university professor and atomic scientist, in an article points out that there is no complete agreement on any scientific theory of the origin of the universe.[37] As Schweitzer suggests, it is "well to be reminded that the Bible's major aim is to tell us who made the universe, and not how it was made."[38] What the chapters do relate is that God created the world and man, that man is dependent on God, that he has been estranged from God, and that he needs to be reconciled to God.

Creation Degenerates: Sin in the Individual (3)

Up to this point there has been unbroken fellowship with God. From chapter 3 on there is a picture of God's pursuing man, wooing him back. The Fall introduces us to man's need and God's grace. This story of sin provides the groundwork for all Christian theology. It shows the *need* for redemption; man himself is helpless to stand before God by virtue of the fact that he characteristically has overstepped the boundary of his creaturehood.

3:1-11. The serpent in the chapter is representative of the powers of evil. In nearly all of Babylonian literature, likewise, dragons and serpents were thought to inhabit the *tehom* (deep) and were thought to be the embodiment of evil. Genesis 3 is not an explanation of the origin of evil. Evil was already here before the serpent spoke. Evil is to be identified with the serpent. It is clear that the source of sin was not from God or from God's nature. The chapter has nothing to say about the source of sin; it does say that sin is here and that all mankind is its victim.

It might be well to remember that this is a different source from that of chapter 1, which says that "God saw all that he had made and it was good." Thus, the writer is not now saying that God made something good and it got out of con-

---

[37]George K. Schweitzer, "The Origin of the Universe," *Review and Expositor,* LIV (April, 1957), 178-194.
[38]*Ibid.,* pp. 188-189.

trol. Both writers are disinterested in explaining the process. They simply endeavor to show something to be characteristic of us all—*we* are sinners! How, why, and where the chapters do not say. One must be satisfied to allow some things to go unexplained, else his is not a religion of faith.

A twofold method was used in leading woman to sin. This is characteristic of the beginning of sin and its control of life—sin which "in the beginning seems full sweet but in the end biteth like an adder." Sin came through an insinuating question, "Did God really [*'aph*] say . . . ?" So often sin's approach is to arouse doubt as to the goodness of God. The question "Did God really say, 'You shall not eat of any tree of the garden'?" implies that it was *unfair* that God should make such a prohibition, selfishly keeping back something that Eve should know. This raised a question as to the integrity of God (3:3), which in turn led to the damaging of Eve's integrity. God had not said that touching the fruit was prohibited; but he had said that if Adam and Eve ate of it, they emphatically would die. Eve reported that they *might* die (a difference between the emphatic and the subjunctive, 2:17 to 3:3). The sin was both in adding to and in altering God's command. "For God knows," an *insinuating statement,* continues the suggestion that God is jealous and is trying to keep man suppressed. This is followed by the suggestion that man can be as God (3:5). At this point, the compiler has placed his finger on the basic human sin—pride, the desire to acknowledge no one as lord but man himself. Man wanted to become equal with God, thus overstepping his creaturehood.

Embodied in the encounter is a summary of sin's appeal to every man—an appeal to the physical and material (good for food), an appeal to vanity (pleasant to the eyes), and a promise of greater knowledge and power through the experience of evil.

The inspired writer wanted to make it plain that sin characteristically and universally involves results and consequences.

Immediately following Eve's sin was a social consequence—
she involved her husband (3:6). To sin alone is enough, but
to involve another is certainly to be haunted by a sense of
inward guilt (3:7). Having lost their inner goodness, early
man and woman tried to compensate by external covering; but
that which is simply outward can never atone.

The futility of human effort at redemption is depicted
through the fig leaves, too small and not very suitable for the
purpose, even though they were among the largest leaves
available in that part of the world. It has been suggested that
the sewing of the fig leaves is only an etiological explanation
of how clothes came to be manufactured and used.[39] But it is
far more. A preachment is underscored; the consequence of
sin is not only the break in man's relationship with God (man
hides from God) but also the break in the pure, natural
harmony between the sexes (man feels shame). To sin and
attempt to shake one's self from dependence upon God is to
disrupt the harmony of God's creation.

With every dark picture in the Old Testament, there is a
bright one. Sin is not the normal relationship, for God constantly seeks man to fellowship with him (3:8). God visited
Adam and Eve in the cool of the day, hinting at the fellowship
which he enjoyed with man prior to his sin. Of course the
language used here is highly anthropomorphic; the picture of
God's walking in the Garden is a graphic description of the
inward experience in the conscience of man.

3:12-24. Regardless of whether man is willing to accept
responsibility for his sin (both Adam and Eve refused, 3:
12-13), he is responsible. For woman the punishment was
painful and difficult childbirth, for sin disrupts the harmony
of God's creation. In addition, her desire was to be toward
her husband, who would exercise tyrannical domination over
her (3:16). It is important to note again that these things

---

[39]W. H. Bennett (ed.), *Genesis*, Vol. I: *The New Century Bible* (Edinburgh:
T. C. & E. C. Jack, n.d.), p. 107.

are perversions of what was intended. When a right relationship with God is established, as much of this as possible should be removed and rectified. Today the validity of such understanding is being championed by the medical profession, which recognizes some possibilities for "painless" childbirth when the mother is emotionally mature.

Man's punishment involved a curse upon the soil. The curse was not work, which had been commanded previous to man's sin (2:15). It was the lack of reward for work, the increasing difficulty of work, and the decreasing productivity of the soil which punishment brought. This continues the theme of sin's bringing disharmony to God's creation.

The severity of the punishment was climaxed in the picture of expulsion from the Garden. Man had snatched a prerogative not meant for him; he had violated the test of obedience (3:24). The purpose of this guardianship is not to keep man out but rather to keep sinful man from approaching God in an unworthy manner. Perhaps this is suggested by the flaming sword, fire so often in the Old Testament being indicative of purity. It does not take unusual insight, thus, to see the truth of someone's appraisal that from the sin of the first man in the Garden to the atoning death of the Son of man on Calvary's cross, sin has left its stream of suffering.

Now for a moment, a backward reflection is needed to consider 3:15, often called the "protevangelium." The idea in the verse is that there shall be one who will use every opportunity to strike at evil—at its most vulnerable spot, represented by the head of the serpent. On the other hand, evil will always be lurking, trying to strike at righteousness, represented by the closest spot to which a serpent could get—the heel. The principle involved is that struggle will ensue to keep man from having again this idyllic fellowship with God. This does not specifically prophesy the Messiah, yet it is in a sense messianic. Here is a picture of the continual conflict which was climaxed on the cross, when it was shown once for all time that victory

can be won and that idyllic fellowship is possible. The translation of 3:15 is dramatic, "A head, he will lie in wait for thee
and enmity a heel, you will lie in wait for him."

The failure to conform to God's purpose is represented in
chapter 3 in the form of poetic symbolism, or parable, with
the intention of illustrating that all mankind has missed the
purpose which God intended for it to fulfil. The serpent is
the personification of the grueling temptation which strikes
at every man—the temptation to assert one's self and drive the
vehicle of life without regard to the demands of obedience to
God.

The opening of the eyes of Adam and Eve (3:7) is the picturesque portrayal of the gnawing, haunting consciousness of
sin—the guilt printed on every man's soul when he sins. The
remainder of the chapter (3:8-24) pictures the unhappiness
which has come to man because he failed to carry out God's
purpose for his life. Also, it points out that the penalty for
failure to perform the God-given purpose is the sentence of
death.[40] Thus, man, as symbolized by being shut out of the
Garden, is really unfit, unworthy to enjoy the blessings of
God. Here is man's predicament. Here is what Tillich has
called "man's passage into non-being";[41] and only a change in
being, an act of new creation, can bring him back again.

Who can fail to see in this presentation numerous pene-
trating concepts? Temptation is an occasion for sin. Freedom
of choice may express itself in sin, which basically is disobedi-
ence or rebellion against God. But let man's inability to take
care of his own sin be known. Man cannot approach God in
an unworthy manner.

All of this is disclosed in a continual conflict between good
and evil.

---

[40]Richardson, *op. cit.*, pp. 76 f.
[41]Paul Tillich, *Systematic Theology* (Chicago: University of Chicago Press,
1951), I, 186-189.

2. The Sociological Implications of Sin (4-5)

The theme of Genesis 4-5 is that "none of us liveth to himself, and no man dieth to himself." The picture of chapter 3 is the marring of man's relationship with God. The story of Cain and Abel, leading to a complex civilization and struggle (4:23), illustrates another thing common to human life—when one's relationship with God his Father is marred, then a tear in his relationship with his brother is not far behind. Here it is demonstrated that life is composed both of a vertical and a horizontal relationship, and sin distorts them both. Sin cannot be kept to itself; it mars the basic relationships of life.

Sin and Conflict, Man to Man (4)

Though there are similar stories in Sumerian literature, such as *Emesh and Entin* and the *Dispute between the Shepherd God and the Farmer God,* the purpose of the Genesis account is unique.

Divided into three sections, the J source speaks of the conflict of Cain and Abel (1-16), the Cainite genealogy (17-24), and the Sethite genealogy (25-26) in an effort to record the origin of the various arts and industries and to record the rapid development of sin. Some might suggest that a subpurpose is to give the reason the Kenites, at times called Cainites (Num. 24:22), came to be wandering nomads in the South. However, it is hardly likely that they would have told such an unfavorable story about themselves. Furthermore, it is doubtful that these stories could be tribal, for there is nothing which could connect the name of Abel with any tribe. There are other purposes in the story, such as supplying an answer as to when sacrifices began, showing the mercy of Yahweh (Cain's mark of protection), demonstrating the judgment of Yahweh (Cain as an outcast), and giving early teaching on the responsibility man has to his brother.

4:1-5. Names for the two characters in the story were

bestowed by the mother. This may be an indication of the early age of the passage, for in a later Hebrew age the children usually were named by the father (cf. Gen. 21:3).

Cain's name means "possession," characteristic of the cry which his mother uttered when the child was born, "I have gotten a man from the Lord" (4:1). The Revised Standard Version translation "with the help of" is paraphrastic. Apparently, she was expressing the great joy which should always accompany childbirth—the joy of participating with God in giving birth to life. This principle is constantly taught in the Scriptures (cf. Psalms 127:3; 128; 139:13). The sovereignty of God is also stressed, for the direct act of God is seen in each birth since it is he who opens the womb (Gen. 4:1,25).

Abel's name means "frailty" or "vanity." For some reason, Eve seems to have been disappointed, and the disappointment is reflected in the name given to the child. It is remotely possible that the name was given to the second son by the editor as a means of conveying the theme in the story of pitting physical strength against physical weakness. There is nothing to recommend the suggestion of Nachmanides (A.D. 1194) that the two names were for the purpose of saying that "man's hold [possession] on this world is vanity."[1]

Representing the agricultural civilizations of the earth, Cain, by occupation a tiller of ground, was perhaps trying to remove the curse of the soil. On the other hand, Abel personifying the nomad herdsman, was a keeper of the sheep. The conflict of Cain and Abel signifies the conflict of two normally compatible parts of creation, another result of sin.

Note that from the beginning, an offering to God is the natural thing, and this was long before the institution of sacrifice by Moses. The author just assumes the existence of altars without giving any account of their origin, another indication that this is an effort at theological history rather than factual history.

---

[1]Cohen, *op. cit.*, p. 17.

Cain's gift of produce was not well received although Abel's offering of his flock was. God had respect for Abel's offering; he approved and accepted it, but he did not respect Cain's. As Calvin once suggested, Cain inferred this, not from the way the smoke went upward or because fire came down and consumed one and not the other, but from the subsequent turn of events.

Entering into the acceptance and nonacceptance was the matter of attitude. Certainly there was some degree of sincerity on the part of both men. The key, however, is that Abel brought the very first and best. The word used for his offering was firstling or "best of the flock." It comes from a root which indicates something very carefully chosen.

Abel recognized himself as God's slave with God as the master to whom the first and the best should be given. Cain simply gave a token to show that he was grateful for services received; he felt it was the thing to do, much in the spirit of tipping the porter for carrying the bags. The term used for "gift" in the text will permit such an interpretation. The word was often used of a gift offered to a superior to express gratitude for one's good will, such as the "meal offering" of thanksgiving at a later time (Lev. 2:1). On the other hand, at times the word was used of a tribute expected from a tributary people such as in 2 Samuel 8:2,6; 1 Kings 5:1; 2 Kings 17:4; and Psalm 72:10.

Cain may have given a little grudgingly, as though he were forced to do so by his superior, very much the way some folk give the tithe. The lesson underscored is that a gift, regardless of what, or how large or small, is a blessing to the giver only if his heart is right as he gives. Here, the essence of religion is implied—giving God the *very best*.

Chapter 4 is an indication, even at this early date, that what God requires is "to do well" and not simply sacrifice (cf. 1 Sam. 12). The same theme is to be seen in the prophetic literature (cf. Amos 5:15; Mic. 6:8; Isa. 1:17; and Jer. 7:5,22).

This matter of the importance of disposition is continued in Genesis 6:5 and 8:21. There is no doubt about the importance of disposition in the Pentateuch when one gets to Leviticus 19:17, "Thou shalt not hate thy brother *in thine heart.*" The correct answer to the acceptance of the offering is to be seen in what has been suggested above and not in any theory of the blood versus the nonblood offering, for the laws on sacrifice had not been instituted yet.

4:6-10. This interpretation with reference to the gifts is confirmed in Cain's reaction to God. His extreme anger indicated that his heart never was right. Had his attitude been proper, Cain would have sought the source of his difficulty. This gives proof to someone's statement that a crisis does not make one lose his faith; it brings out what faith one has—or does not have.

A retranslation of 4:7 makes clearer the purpose. "If thou doest well, shall there not be a lifting up [of thy countenance] and if thou doest not well, sin is crouching." Sin crouches at the door like a wild beast ready to devour. You must control it. The Lord urges Cain to conquer the wild beast of hate before it springs to murder. In other words, unless sin is taken to God and straightened out, it lies at the door of man's heart, continually working on it. Be careful, or you will add more sin to what you have done. Cain did not control his hate. It looks as though Cain started a conversation with Abel to draw him into a quarrel (4:8). The murder was done in the field away from the parents' presence.[2]

To be human is to be responsible to God, and to be responsible to God is to be responsible to one's brother. All are important to God; consequently, the totality of relationship is important. In 3:9 God had asked, "Where art thou?"; and in 4:9 he has to ask, "Where is Abel?" Such is the path of sin.

---

[2]There might be some debate here, for the "let us go into the field" of verse 8 is missing in the Hebrew. It is, however, included in the Samaritan Pentateuch, the Septuagint, and the Vulgate.

A wrong relationship with God expresses itself in a wrong relationship with our brothers—the second is the result of the first. Cain's answer (4:9*b*) "Am I my brother's keeper?" was a poor one. It was an implication that he had no responsibility to his brother, a cry modern business and society often use. But there is no escape from the sociological implications of sin.

4:11-16. Sin's infectious contamination of all society is not without its parallels of judgment and mercy. Besides being a fugitive, Cain's fate was to live on a land that was no longer productive. This was stringent judgment, for the worst punishment a farmer can have is to have his ground fail or to lose his ground. In all of the Old Testament there is a direct relationship between a blessed life and a blessed land. Apparently, Cain's happy-go-lucky attitude was not deep-seated, for his immediate response to his judgment was a plea for aid (4: 13-14). He was worried about his relationship with man (4:14). For him to have been so concerned, there must have been other people in the world; thus, *'adam* originally must have meant "mankind," not just one person. His present relationship with God was equally disturbing to Cain. "From thy face shall I be hid" (4:14) enunciates a principle that all men need to learn. Sin shuts man out from the presence of God. Within his being there was hunger for God, but Cain had been careless about his relationship. This is as modern as today.

God's judgment is ever tempered by his mercy. When Cain made a plea for aid, God promised to place a mark of protection on him (usually presented as on his forehead in pictorial representation) so that whoever saw Cain would know not to molest him. It is tragic that this verse has been prostituted so often and interpreted as the initiation of the Negro race, the result of the mark. This mark is not a curse; it is a sign of God's protection, special providence, grace, and mercy. Whether the mark was part of the literary imagination, or actual, it is impossible to know. Someone has suggested that the figure was similar to that with which slaves were often branded. The mark would designate Cain as the "slave of God." This may be corroborated in that the name Cain resembles the Arabic *Gain-el* ("slave of God"). The sevenfold vengeance which was to fall on those who molested Cain seems to have occupied quite a place in ancient Hebrew thought. Perhaps this is why the disciple thought himself most magnanimous when he asked if he should forgive seven times (Matt. 18:21). The sevenfold vengeance idea is seen in the execution of seven of Saul's family (2 Sam. 21:8). It is a rather primitive idea, but the truth underlying the use of the figure here is that God would judge those who bothered one under his protection. He cares for his own.

The place to which Cain went, the land of Nod (4:16), cannot be located geographically. "Nod" means "wander," and, perhaps, indicates a seminomadic life. At any rate, it introduces a new pace in man's activities, and there follows a brief glimpse at the origin of the principal arts and institutions of civilized life. Connected with this development is the theme that the advance of civilization does not necessarily make man more Godlike. Indeed, the more man developed his ability to be partially self-sustaining, the less attention he gave to his fellowship with God.

4:17-26. Illustrating the principle that as civilization increases, spirituality decreases, the author gives a glimpse at illustrative examples. Enoch was the first city builder (4:17b) while Lamech was the first to practice polygamy (4:19). The city gave birth to such evil. Sons of Lamech engaged in various activities (4:20). Jabal was the father of the bedouin type of people. Rashi, Jewish rabbi and scholar of A.D. 1040, reported that tradition held Jabal to be the first to build temples for idols. Jubal was the father of music and, according to Rashi, was the first to introduce music into the service of idolatry. Tubal-cain was an ironsmith. In addition to picturing the various activities of man, whoever suggested that Cain's line was trying to compensate for its loss of God was right. Civilization's turmoil when it follows such action (4:23) is to violate its relationship with God and man by taking revenge in its own hands. This is the end of every godless civilization, overconfident because of its metals and weapons. But gloom and light are often woven together. God does not leave himself without a witness. Civilization's hope can be seen in the continuation of a godly line (4:25-26). From the beginning there has been somewhere a remnant separated to the worship of God. There will be a people of God set in the midst of the world.

Sin and Conflict, God and Man (5)

This is the P account which mainly gives the genealogy from Adam to Noah, a different edition of the Cainite genealogy. There is a striking similarity between verses 1-3 and the first chapter of Genesis, which is also the Priestly source. It is interesting that he "named *them* man ['*adam*] when they were created," another indication of P's concept that God created "mankind." Verse 3 is an important one, for it shows that the image of God was not obliterated by the Fall. The image of God was transmitted to Seth and his posterity.

The particular problem of chapter 5 is the longevity of the antediluvians. Various theories have been suggested, and it is impossible to be absolutely definite about any approach. It is difficult to believe that they actually lived as long as stated. Nachmanides said that the men lived this long because they were physically perfect and that it was only after the Flood that physical deterioration set in. A study of 187 Neanderthal fossils from the upper Paleolithic (100000) and Neolithic (10000) ages shows that only 3 of these passed the age of fifty; 13 died between the ages of forty to fifty, one-third died before reaching twenty, and the remainder died between the ages of twenty to forty.[3] Research indicates short lives for the

---

[3]Lincoln Barnett, "The Dawn of Religion," *Life*, XXXIX (December 12, 1955).

ancient men rather than long ones. It is only in comparatively recent times that longevity has increased. An effort has been made to remove the difficulty by considering the names as those of dynasties, families, or tribes and not as individuals. Each name would stand for a group rather than for an individual. Thus, given in the chapter is the period when the family held prominence. However, there is nothing in the context to indicate that the names are other than individual names. It would be better to consider the names as individual names, with many having been omitted, the large ages including also the years for those names omitted. Another line of reasoning is with reference to the term for "years," (*shanah*). It is conjectured that perhaps *shanah* means "months" rather than years; i.e. that a different translation for *shanah* would lower the ages. However, if this plan were followed, it would make Methuselah approximately five years of age when he himself had a son, a physical and practical improbability. Also invalidating this suggestion is the fact that a passage in close proximity, Genesis 7:11, uses the term *shanah* in connection with *chodesh* (month) and *yom* (day); and the division of time in the verse demands the translation "year" for *shanah*. Finally, although it is presented with some reluctance, there does seem to be an emphasis here which is in keeping with the larger purpose of the Priestly source. In all probability, the Priestly writer simply exaggerated the ages in order to show the glory of an ancient civilization. Mesopotamian and Babylonian stories leading to the depiction of the Flood have a similar ten antediluvians with exceedingly long ages, often thousands of years older than any of the men mentioned here in Genesis 5. The long ages of P are then an exaggerated literary medium for the purpose of expressing the view that sin brings degeneration.

Practically the only highlight of the chapter, with the exception of the Enoch passage, is the monotonous "he lived, he begat, he died." Typical of modern life, which often leaves little behind in the way of genuine contribution, this section with its characters sometimes has been called "the history of nobodyism." But like a fruitful bough in a barren place is 5:24, "Enoch walked with God; and he was not; for God took him." The close fellowship with God began when Methuselah, Enoch's first child, was born (5:22). Certainly, it is at such a time that one realizes the need of a closer walk with God. It is an intensely privileged responsibility to care for human life.

The expression "walked with God" signifies intimate fellowship and companionship. The verb *halak* is so used again in 1 Samuel 25:15 to depict the contact between David's messengers and the servants of Abigail. In this instance in Genesis, a morally and religiously mature commitment is involved. The *hithpael* form of the verb (*wayith halek*) is used here, denoting a reflexive relationship. They "walked" back and forth together. This must not have been easy for Enoch, for he was a contemporary of Lamech, who was the epitome of evil. Only one generation followed, and the Flood came. Enoch is an example of the ability to uphold the banner of righteousness, even in an evil age. Since much emphasis has been given to the promises of materialistic and temporal reward in the Old Testament, it is important to note that Enoch's righteousness was not accompanied by any outward change of circumstance. He did not become wealthy nor was he blessed with any special talents or powers. He was just an ordinary man.

"God took him" is not necessarily an indication that he disappeared suddenly and was nowhere to be found. It is the Old Testament's expression of belief in the ideal of immortality. Death is not a cessation of being, but it is a change in one's place of abode. This is the Old Testament's hint of the reality expressed in John 14. The position of this emphasis just before the Flood is important, for it suggests that God rewards the faithful and the righteous, thereby making it possible to get to the tree of life. A hint of grace and of optimism brightens the picture made so dark by chapter 3.

3. Man's Wickedness and God's Judgment (6:1 to 11:25)

That the inherent evil in all men (6:5) deserves judgment and that this judgment comes, as seen in the Flood story, is the theme of this block of material. Though wickedness brings judgment, it is judgment tempered with mercy and grace, as seen in the deliverance of Noah and his family. The entire episode is calculated to say that it is God who engineers deliverance and salvation, but even God's help often is unappreciated. Something drastic must happen to man.

Introduction to the Flood (6:1-8)

The story of the marriage of the sons of God with the daughters of men and the consequent announcement of doomed existence is placed here specifically to show the end result of sin—judgment—and to serve as a prelude and introduction to the Flood. A consideration of the terms involved is perhaps the best way of seeing the passage's significance.

"Sons of God" suggests several possibilities, especially since "sons of" may mean "belonging to the class of." Often the term seems to imply semidivine, angelic beings who frequent the court of heaven. In some passages, the phrase definitely refers to such beings.[1] On the other hand, the term could mean, simply, godly or God-fearing sons, perhaps from the line of Seth. A further suggestion is that the phrase indicates royal people of noble birth. Paralleling this last suggestion, the interpreter would view "daughters of men" as referring to people of lowly birth. However, there seems to be nothing in the context to suggest class distinction. A second suggestion is that the "daughters of men" were beautiful though sinful

---

[1]Cf. Job 1:6; Dan. 3:25; Psalm 89:6.

women, perhaps from Cain's line. A further term which needs clarification is the term "mighty ones," "giants," or *nephilim* in 6:4. The root is *naphal*, "to fall"; thus, the *nephilim* are the "fallen ones." Other passages make reference to unusual men and imply that they were unusual with reference to size. Numbers 13:33 actually uses the term *nephilim* and in some sense equates them with the sons of Anak, or Anakim. Deuteronomy 1:28; 2:10-11,21; 9:2; and Joshua 15:14 do not use the term *nephilim* but speak of the men as sons of Anak, or Anakim; so the group referred to includes the *nephilim*. In spite of this, it must not be concluded that *nephilim* originally meant "giants." There may have been a tradition of the "fallen ones" from an early date, and across the years the "fallen ones" and "giants" were associated together. Some *nephilim* may have been small in stature, while others may have been large. To help place the *nephilim*, many would suggest that as a closing part to verse 2, there originally was the phrase "they conceived and bore the *nephilim*," but that somehow across the years it was dropped out of the text.

According to Skinner, other literature frequently recorded the marriage of gods with mortals. On that basis, it may be that the theme here is of the actual marriage of angels with human beings.[2] However, there is no record elsewhere in the Scriptures that this actually happened. In addition, there is a major difference in this story and that of mythology. In mythology, the sons of the gods came down for their own gratification; whereas, in the biblical contexts, when the sons of God were active, they were servants, obedient unto death for the purpose, not of lowering, but of raising and helping those on earth. The proper perspective is some sense in which the interpretation of the godly and the ungodly's marrying is to be connected with mythology. The author has perhaps used a fragment of mythology as a literary vehicle to "convey the sense of what theologians call the 'demonic,' i.e., the potentiali-

---

[2]Skinner, *op. cit.*, p. 140.

ties of the human race for heroic good or spectacular evil."
Thus, the idea of the marriage was borrowed from mythology
as a means of underscoring the evil and demonic in man and
was not intended to be taken literally. This symbolic significance portrays a truth far more pertinent than a factual event
could portray. Something of the purpose of this introductory
section in chapter 6 can be seen. It simply expands chapter 3
and its emphasis that sin is in the world. The demonic feature
in man necessitates that his days be numbered.[3] From the
idea that sin came because of demonic forces outside man, it
is interesting to note that in Job 1, Satan was among the sons
of God. Thus, those evil forces in God's world outside man
caused sin in man. Man gave in and a sinful world resulted.
Placed here as an introduction to the Flood, it shows the reason for the Flood—the sin of man and the demonic principle
of sin on the earth.

6:3. "My spirit shall not always strive with man." "My
spirit shall not abide in man for ever" (RSV).

Ruach, as used in this passage, has been conjectured to be
an ethical principle striving against the corruption of men
or divine feeling excited by human sin or the divine principle
of life implanted in man at creation.

"Strive with" is not a good translation for *yadon,* which accompanies *ruach.* The use of it represents a theological presupposition. Various Hebrew roots are possibilities. One
choice is *din,* to be obedient or submissive. With the negative, the resultant translation would read, "My spirit shall not
be humbled." A second possibility is the middle vowel verb
don, to dwell or abide, while perhaps the best choice of all is
the Akkadian, or Aramaic root, *nadan,* which means to expiate
for or to shield or protect.[4] This particular root is used as a
noun in 1 Chronicles 21:7 and as a verb in Daniel 7:15. In
the Chronicles passage the noun is a "sheath," i.e., a protector

---

[3]Richardson, *op. cit.,* p. 94.
[4]Brown, Driver, and Briggs, *op. cit.,* p. 623.

for a sword. Using something of the nominal meaning in the verb form, one would phrase the passage, "My spirit shall not protect man forever."

Thus, the passage seems to be a matter of God's unwillingness any longer to shoulder either man's behavior or the consequences of man's behavior. The announcement of 6:3 is that God will not indefinitely shield or protect the guilty. There must be a time of definite reckoning for sin. It would seem, then, that the verb, as used in this particular context, includes both the first meaning of "being humbled" and protection. Let it be noticed, however, that this does not mean that God is going to stop man's opportunity. As long as there is breath, there is hope. God continues to call and to grant man opportunity, although man can continue to walk so long in the opposite direction from God that his ears may fail to receive the call. The 120 years are indicative that God was giving a short time before the Flood when his judgment would come. In relation to the long time they have survived previously, there is to be only a short time before judgment.

6:4. Although difficult in the Hebrew, apparently, the verse means to imply that these mighty men arose as a consequence of the union of the divine and the human, the good and the bad. There is some internal evidence for the inclusion of the suggested phrase of verse 2, "they conceived and bore the *nephilim.*"

6:5. The moral constitution of man's entire nature is corrupt. Sin is not something on the surface to be easily cleared. Since every imagination of man's heart was evil, there was in the future no hope of repentance unless some radical change was introduced.

6:6. "And it repented the Lord that he had made man on the earth." "And the Lord was sorry that he had made man on the earth" (RSV).

Translated as it is, this verse portrays God as changeable in nature and with misgivings about the goodness and validity of his creation. Aside from a very serious charge against the character of God and a dilemma of theology, linguistically the translation must not stand.

The verb translated here as "repented" or "sorry" is the verb *nacham*, which basically means to be moved with great emotion or concern, to have inward feeling about something.[5] This intense concern or feeling might take several directions—repentance, sorrow, concern, comfort, love, be grieved in the heart. Thus, to suggest that the Lord was grieved in the heart because he had made man is to suggest anthropomorphically that he heaved a sigh; that is, he was greatly disturbed about the man whom he had created. He had not changed his purpose, nor was he sorry, nor did he feel that he had made a mistake in creating man. Rather, it grieved the Lord that man had behaved as he had. This is an expression of God's concern and compassion for man.

6:7-8. The only alternative was for God manifestly to use his sovereignty in dramatic fashion, both as an act of judgment, punishing the sinners, and as an act of mercy, allowing such as Noah and his family to escape. Again, the two great principles of God's revelation, judgment and mercy, are in focus.

Noah and the Flood (6:9 to 9:29)

Before a look is taken at some of the externals of the story, it might be helpful to notice that Noah found acceptance before God because of his righteousness. His deeds and life found favor in God's sight. This is a striking contrast to contemporary flood accounts, where any salvation was simply through the capricious choice of the gods. Testimony to Noah's righteousness is the word *tam* (6:9), sometimes translated "blameless," or as the Revised Standard Version has it,

---

[5] Cf. Brown, Driver, and Briggs, *op. cit.*, and *Gesenius' Hebrew and Chaldee Lexicon*, trans. Samuel Prideaux Tregelles (Grand Rapids: Wm. B. Eerdman's Publishing Co., 1957).

"perfect." However, the word does not imply perfection. According to the Hebrew root, it simply means that Noah was mature, loyal, or complete in his allegiance to God. He had the kind of relationship with God that God expected.

There have been numerous flood legends throughout various parts of the earth. Even the American Indians are reported to have a flood story with characters whose names are similar to those of Noah and his family. The Chinese have a legend relating to the Yellow River, dated about 2298 B.C.; and, of course, there is the very familiar Gilgamesh epic, in which Utnapishtim is the hero. Other flood stories are related to Persia, Africa, the Ganges; and among the Greeks there is the story of Deucalion, the son of Prometheus, who has his setting in a deluge myth.

The question of the universality of the Flood has occupied scholars for a long time. Searching for flood evidence, Sir Leonard Woolley dug pits in the Mesopotamian region. Though he found some in places, just four miles away at Tell el-Obeid there was none. There seems to be little evidence from science that the Flood was universal. The term "all" in 7:19 may have been used from the standpoint of an observer.

Bernard Ramm has summarized in brief space the three approaches toward understanding the Flood accounts. One of these generally is held by those who approach the story from a local viewpoint. Some have argued that man prior to the Flood did not live outside the Mesopotamian Valley. However, all geologists and anthropologists have accumulated much influence to the contrary. From the opposite direction, and seeking to ameliorate the problem in the previous suggestion, there is the hypothesis that during some early Ice Age man was driven into the Mesopotamian Valley. Finally, and in keeping with the over-all nature of Genesis 1 to 11, the record of a local flood may be understood phenomenally.[6] If

---

[6]Bernard Ramm, *The Christian View of Science and Scripture* (Grand Rapids: Wm. B. Eerdman's Publishing Co., 1955), p. 238.

this view is correct, the Flood was considered in universal terms because it was universal in its religious significance.

It is important to notice that the record neither affirms nor denies that life existed beyond the Mesopotamian area. There is evidence for the existence of men far outside the Mesopotamian Valley; and certainly Noah did not serve as a preacher of warning and righteousness to the far flung people of Africa, India, China, and America (Heb. 11:7). Linguistically, "all" is used throughout the Scriptures as a manner of speaking (cf. Psalm 22:17; Deut. 2:34; 1 Kings 18:20; Matt. 3:5) to indicate a large number; and it is not intended to be "all inclusive."

In the realm of geological evidence there are numerous testimonies to a local flood. Such problems include getting rid of such a vast amount of water, for there would be no place for all of it to drain. As a matter of fact, the Scriptures report that the wind took care of it (8:1).

The total destruction of plant life under such heavy water and the mammoth task of transporting, feeding, and caring for an untold number of animals are other problems to be faced in the universal flood hypothesis.[7] Just think of the equipment, space, and crews needed to operate a city zoo, which does not have representatives of nearly all the fowl and animal life of the world.

All of this suggests that the compiler of Genesis was using a local flood account only as a means of introducing the background and culture out of which the need arose for Abraham to serve as the representative of God.

Much unnecessary attention has been paid to differences in the sources (J and P) from which the Flood account was composed. It cannot be denied that there are two sources, that each source when segregated tells a complete story. The main points of difficulty are with reference to the number of beasts and to the number of days of rain. While the Priestly source

---

[7] *Ibid.*, pp. 245 f.

mentions one pair of (all) beasts (6:17-22), the Yahwistic source presents seven pairs of clean beasts (7:1-5). Although the Yahwistic source states a forty-day rain (7:4), the Priestly source speaks of a one-hundred-fifty-day rain (7:24;8:3). The differences do not discredit the record. They only indicate, once again, that the Old Testament cannot be interpreted truly apart from recognition of the spiritual principle which is conveyed.

The length of the Flood account makes it impractical presently to look at every detail. Therefore, only some of the points of interest will require our attention.

The word for ark (*tevah*) is the same word used for the container in which Moses was saved (Ex. 2:3-5), and it is also the same term used for the ark of testimony (Ex. 25:10) in the worship ritual. This similarity would suggest that *tevah* is an Egyptian loan word. If this be true, it is another indicator that often the Hebrews "baptized" foreign patterns and used them for new purposes. The conception of a vessel 300 by 50 by 30 cubits (525 by 87½ by 52½ feet) was quite a task. The feet measurements are derived from the supposition that a cubit is about 18 to 24 inches, approximately the distance from the tip of the hand to the elbow.

An interesting detail of the story is the statement in 7:16 that "the Lord shut him in." In the Gilgamesh epic, it was Utnapishtim who shut the door of the escape vessel. If Noah himself had controlled the door, he might have admitted people unwisely. This was God's judgment and God's mercy, so he had to control it! Salvation is God's affair under God's control.

Although an act of worship and thanksgiving follows this act of God's mercy (8:20), a theological stake is driven down in 8:21 to imply that the act of worship does not mean that the experience has caused any basic change in man. The statement of 8:21 "the imagination of man's heart is evil from his youth" implies that the descendants of Noah would be no

THE NEED OF MAN

better than their predecessors and verifies this by giving a striking example of depravity in the Noah incident. Sin is characteristic of *all* mankind.

9:1-17. Upon the conclusion of the Flood, several principles are enunciated for the foundation of man's relationships. Some natural disharmony is implied between the man and the animals (9:2). The balance in man and animal's relationship is to be disturbed. Not until mankind's sin problem is straightened out will the proper balance in God's creation exist (Isa. 11:6-9).

Man might push too far in his domination over animal life and forget that all creation is God's. When animal life was killed, care must be taken not to eat blood, for life resides in the blood (Lev. 17:11,14; Deut. 12:23). Consequently, the practice developed that all blood must be drained off before meat could be eaten (Lev. 7:27; 17:10,14). The practice of eating only prepared, or "kosher," meat thus is based on the principle that since God gave life, as represented by the blood, it is not right for man to do any damage to life.

The outcome of the Flood was God's establishment of a covenant of grace which provided sustenance for man (9:11). This involved an anticipated order in society (9:6). The covenant was unconditional, with no requirement laid on man unless the instruction to be fruitful and multiply is part of the covenant.

The symbolism of the covenant was the bow. The bow has been popular in other literature and languages and usually indicates some past event. Among the Indians, the bow was laid aside after a contest with the demons. According to the Arabs, Kujah shot arrows from his bow and then hung his bow in the clouds. In Babylonian literature, Marduk reportedly used the bow against Tiamat and then set the bow in the heavens as a constellation. In the literature of Iceland, the bow served as a bridge between heaven and earth. Similar usage of the bow is to be found in Hebrew imagery. The lightning bolts are Yahweh's arrows; when the storm is over, his bow (cf. Hab. 3:9-11; Psalm 7:12 f.) is laid aside and appears in the sky as a sign that his anger is over. The bow is a weapon of war.

In poetic expression, God laid aside his wrath and placed his bow in the cloud as a sign that toward his creation peace is to reign. God will ever be merciful to all mankind is the message. Man's response in worship had brought God's response in return. God's responsibility was not to destroy by flood, while Noah's responsibility was to respect the sacredness of life as a recognition of God (9:4). In all of this, man was to realize that without God's providence, without the constant covenanted care and protection of God, human life could not continue for any time at all.

9:18-28. Noah at his worst is presented in the next few verses. The Bible paints no superficial, rosy picture but gives both the good and the bad. Tragically, Noah turned the fruit of the soil into a curse, even though part of the function of the Flood seems to have been to remove curse. There was nothing wrong with the vine or with its fruit. As so often is done with God's gifts, Noah perverted his blessings.

Another facet of evil is to be learned. Temptation and sin often strike immediately after victory, when one lowers his defense. From his previous experiences, Noah was secure against old temptations, but relaxation prohibited his seeing the danger of new temptations.

So often man lives as though he is happy when a brother falls, and Ham exhibited a poor attitude in this instance. He rather rejoiced that the old saint, who no doubt had many times given aid to his sons, now needed aid himself.

The end result was a curse (9:25), but the curse is upon Canaan, the son of Ham, and not on Ham. The descendants of Canaan were the Canaanites, who occupied the land of Palestine, while the Hamites seem to have been the forerunners of the Egyptians, Ethiopians, and Abyssinians. Thus, any

suggestion that the curse had to do with race or color must be
rejected immediately, nor is there any suggestion in the passage that God approves a curse. Noah was simply making an
observation.

It is impossible for a boy to avoid hard times and experiences
when he has such an evil father and example as Ham. Thus,
the thought is "Canaan will surely have a curse to bear" and
not "I curse Canaan." Here is something of the influence of
sin on those who follow.

J. Hoftizer has suggested an interpretation of the cursing
from a political standpoint. A previously existent story of the
turmoil of brothers was used to explain the battles for control
of the land of Palestine.[8] It is to be doubted, however, that
the story is politically oriented. It is simply another piece of
the puzzle portraying the disaster of sin and its ramifications.

The Universality of Judgment (10:1 to 11:25)

The God of All Men

It is striking that such an emphasis as that in chapter 10
follows immediately after the making of the Noah covenant
in chapter 9. The emphasis is that God's covenant is with
all men everywhere. This note of universality is accompanied
by a missions note. The tracing of the location of the families
of the earth underscores the conviction that Yahweh is the God
of all the earth and her people. Consequently, there is no
doubt that he is the hope of the Gentiles as well as the Jews.
Also made clear is the principle of election, for it is out of the
great number of the nations of the earth that Israel is selected.

Admittedly, there are many problems in the chapter. Asshur,
who is listed in the Shem phase, verse 22, has already been
listed in the Ham list, verse 11. Note that the Revised Standard Version translated it "Assyria" in verse 11, thus avoiding

---

[8]J. Hoftizer, "Some Remarks to the Tale of Noah's Drunkenness," *Studies on
the Book of Genesis* ("Oudtestamentische Studiën," XII, Leiden: E. J. Brill,
1958), pp. 22-27.

a discrepancy. The Cush-Nimrod passage of verses 8-12 does not seem to belong or harmonize where it is; for it seems improbable that Cush, normally associated with Ethiopia, should be associated with the Assyrian and Babylonian empires.

Havilah and Sheba of the Ham list (verse 7) are listed in verse 28 with the Shem list. The Medo-Persians (Madai), listed in verse 2 in the Japheth group, normally assigned to Asia Minor, Europe, actually belong in the Mesopotamian region (v. 22). This is to say nothing of the fact that the list is not complete. People very prominent elsewhere in the book of Genesis are omitted altogether here. The omission includes such prominent peoples as the Moabites and the Edomites.

Numerous other peculiarities force one to admit that there has been some kind of textual corruption. Nevertheless, definite things are accomplished in the arrangement of the chapter. Canaan is definitely circumscribed as the center of the world map, the place where God was working a work of a supreme importance to all. Geographically, Japheth (Europe, Asia Minor), Ham (area below the Fertile Crescent), and Shem (Mesopotamian region) are placed around Canaan to indicate that the God of the universe must punish the wickedness of all men dwelling everywhere. In the world of sin, the spotlight is focused upon Shem (10:21), who is to pave the pathway to Abraham and righteousness. This ancestry is broken only by the tower of Babel story in the first part of chapter 11.

With relation to the Flood account of the previous chapters, it is significant that chapter 10 says nothing about people outside the local flood area, as though the author had no concern for tracing descendants other than Noah and his sons; and no mention is made of races other than Caucasian, for presumably Noah's sons were all alike.[9]

Supremacy of God over Creation

The tower of Babel parable shows the futility and emptiness

[9]Ramm, *op. cit.*, pp. 337 f.

of human effort divorced from the acknowledgment and service of God. Religiously, the theme involves the desire of man to transcend his divinely affixed place. The chapter thus explains theologically the dispersion of the human race, which is presented in Genesis 10. When man's pride leads him to desire to take over the prerogatives of God, disturbance and dispersion follow.

The statement that the tower reached into the heavens does not mean that men were trying to build something which would give them access into God's heaven. Picturesque language is used here to indicate a building which was so tall that one got dizzy when looking at its height. It was a sort of skyscraper. Many such buildings are built today. When this building was built, however, God punished the people by confusing their language. They could no longer understand one another and thus were scattered so that many of them lost contact with each other. There was something connected with this building which expressed the sin of the people. When people sin, confusion results.

That this building was a Babylonian ziggurat is not stated; but since the building took place in the land of Shinar (Babylon, 11:2), it is a natural assumption. A tall ziggurat could serve as a lookout and as a rallying place for defense. It could be used as a fortress, and with several of these in strategic positions, a city could feel secure. Since the people felt secure with their own fortifications, their need for God would be minimized. The Plain of Shinar was a very prosperous place, and, apparently, they wanted to stay there in order to become great in the eyes of men (11:4). They were concerned with making *their* name great, when they had been created for the purpose of magnifying and giving glory to God. God wanted them, as his stewards, to subdue the earth, but they wanted to stay in one place. Vanity and rebellion were coupled together. Most of the ziggurats had pagan temples on top. The entire affair indicated syncretistic and compromised allegiance to Yahweh. Poor worship brings confusion.

The resultant judgment for having attempted the tower was in their being scattered abroad, the very thing they were trying to prevent. The people spread, and as a result of the lack of contact with each other, the language was confused. Anthropologists generally agree that men once spoke one language but that as they moved to different parts of the earth, peculiarities of language developed. All of this is to say that in spite of the many opportunities which God gave man, man consistently showed himself to be characterized by sin.

Thus, in story form there occurs again a summary description of man's need for redemption. Even when God does his best and offers his best, man's nature is such that he continues in sin. Consequently, the unity of all mankind, in all of life's relations, continues to be shattered by sin so that the lack of ability to understand, confusion, and turmoil encompass the earth. Could there be any better concluding summary or emphasis than this—that man stands in the need of something or somebody to rescue him from his confused, wandering existence?

George Ernest Wright climaxes the matter when he suggests that one cannot assume that the inspired compiler and editor of the traditions had no answer to the distressing problems which this perspective of human history reveals.[10] Thus must follow the account of God's election of one to convey a way of meeting man's needs.

---

[10] G. Ernest Wright, *The Old Testament Against Its Environment* ("Studies in Biblical Theology," No. 2; Chicago: Alec R. Allenson, Inc., 1950), pp. 52 ff.

Part III

God's Answer
to Man's Need

4. Man as God's Instrument (11:26 to 25:11)

Introduction

Coming after the exposé of sin in chapters 1-11, this section shows God's selection of a man to bear his message of redemption. From Abraham, the chosen one, would be a people, the Hebrews; and from them the message of redemption would be made known to the entire world.

One should be aware as he approaches the remaining chapters in Genesis that with chapter 12 a transition is made in the nature of the material. The second half of Genesis records a less parabolic and more detailed historical account of the lives of various individuals and the places which they fulfilled in the providence of God. That all do not agree that this is true of the patriarchal narratives can perhaps best be clarified through a statement from S. H. Hooke:

Twenty years or so ago, I was inclined to see in the eighth century prophets the true founders of the religion of Israel. I thought that Abraham was too misty a figure of saga to have any real significance for the history of Israel's religion, and that, while I accepted Moses as an historical figure, so much legendary material had accumulated round him, and so much of the legislation ascribed to him was clearly either of a later date, or dependent on an earlier common stock of Semitic law and custom, that I discounted his importance for the founding of the corporate religion of what was ultimately to be Israel. In this now I believe I was mistaken. In the first place, the more I admitted the existence of those elements in the early development of Israel's religion of which I have already spoken, the more it became necessary to account for the fact that Israel's history did not peter out like that of the other small nations around her, but became the vehicle of the unique revelation of God. The emergence of the eighth century prophets was a religious phenomenon which itself called for an explanation. So I came to see in the tradition of the double call and choice of Israel in Abraham and in Moses an authentic tradition of a profound religious experience. . . .

So it seemed to me that one had to acknowledge that at the beginning, in the experience of Abraham and Moses, a flame was kindled which was never to be extinguished.[1]

Along with Hooke, the present writer's contention is that the material is historical. Thus, the prophets of a later age were not innovators but reformers, or revivalists, calling the people of Israel back to the faith of the patriarchs.[2]

Much fact and theory have made the question of the historicity of the patriarchs a tedious one. However, in the New Testament, both Jesus and the disciples bear testimony to the greatness and, consequently in the mind of the present writer, to the historicity of the patriarchs.

There are at least 139 references in the Bible to Abraham as an individual; 60 of these are New Testament references. For example, in John 8:31-44 the Jews were claiming racial lineage from Abraham. Jesus told them that if they were Abraham's children, they would do what Abraham did. Then Jesus said that they were of their father the devil because they did not believe as Abraham believed. This appears to be a remark indicating historicity and not just a reference of accommodation.

Stephen, in Acts 7, was preaching the sermon which led to his martyrdom. He recited the call and the faith of Abraham

---

[1]Hooke, *The Siege Perilous,* pp. 182-183.
[2]*Ibid.*

and mentioned him in connection with Isaac and Jacob. Stephen cited these early days as history.

Paul was a Hebrew of the Hebrews; and both before and after his conversion he believed that Abraham *was,* and referred to him as the supreme example of faith (e.g., Gal. 3). Indeed, he used him to illustrate the entire philosophy of Christian belief. It is hardly likely that he would have built so much upon a nonexistent one. As is so vividly seen in Hebrews 11, whoever wrote the book of Hebrews believed that Abraham was more than a legend and had no hesitancy in using both him and Sarah and other patriarchs as actual heroes of faith, while James (James 2:21-24) in seeking to demonstrate the working out of one's faith and the characteristics of a Christian's work likewise could point to no better example than Abraham.

There is little doubt about the New Testament acceptance of Abraham and the other patriarchs as historical and that the stories surrounding their lives are essentially accurate. Nevertheless, various approaches need to be considered; for although most of them were suggested in the material of the late 1800's and early 1900's, some of them still persist.

For a long time the theory was popular which held that the patriarchs were eponymous ancestors. Eponym (name upon), from the Greek *epi* (upon) and *onoma* (name), usually indicates a name or phrase formed from the name of a person to designate a people. Thus, it has been suggested that Abraham was a person invented so as to give some background to the Hebrew people, or to show how a clan got its name.

Another twist to the eponymous suggestion is that the names now known as individual patriarchs were originally the names of tribes or clans. The basic objection is to be seen in the fact that no tribe or people takes its name from Abraham, for instance. Furthermore, since the patriarchs are presented as individuals, to take this position is to indicate a deliberate fraud or lie on the part of the Scripture writers.

A suggestion similar to it is indicated under the terminology, "clan figure." This is the suggestion that Abraham was not an individual at all but represented the movements of the Hebrew people as a racial group. C. A. Simpson summarizes the concept:

Historically this unique relationship began not with the response of one man, Abraham, to an explicit divine call, but in a collective response by the group, then or later known as the sons of Israel, to external reality manifesting itself in the thunderstorm and the volcano[?] of Sinai.[3]

Aside from the manipulation of the Scriptures involved, to develop an individual from a race rather than a race from an individual is more complex and illogical. There is little reason today to feel, as the opinion of Simpson assumes, that the patriarchal traditions simply reflect the conditions and manufacturings of the monarchy (tenth to the seventh centuries B.C.).

Far worse is the suggestion that the patriarchs were originally pagan deities by these names who gradually were lowered to the status of human heroes. Although it was first suggested that these deities later reduced to men were the creation of native Hebrew mythology, under the influence of Winckler and Meyer, the theory was propounded that this was the adaptation of Canaanite influence. As will be seen shortly, there is too much archaeological material from Mari and Nuzi to dismiss the patriarchs as pagan deities reduced to human size.[4]

A frequent proposal of scholars is that the stories of the patriarchs are simply popular folk tales about the greatness of the ancestors, legendary narratives such as are common to all people in all places. Gradually they became localized and

---

[3]C. A. Simpson, "The Book of Genesis," *The Interpreters Bible* (ed.), Nolan B. Harmon (New York: Abingdon-Cokesbury Press, 1952), I, 440.

[4]Skinner, *op. cit.*, pp. xxxiv-xlii.

were applied to the Hebrew people and, consequently, were given Hebrew characters and names so as to better carry out the patriotism of the Hebrew people. However, before legends arise there must be some historical fact or personage around which or whom the legends can develop. The historical individual becomes the basis for legends, not vice versa. It would also be next to impossible under the above theory to explain how such varied stories became associated with individual names.

Two kindred proposals are the "cult myth" and the "etymological myth" explanation. Under the "cult myth" suggestion, the stories are inventions so as to explain the sacredness of the revered sanctuaries and ritual customs such as in chapters 16, 18, 28 and the Genesis 17 passage on circumcision. To view the stories as "etymological myths" is to suggest that they are an effort to analyze or explain how certain people got their names.[5]

Perhaps before any detailed statement of evidence has been presented, it already has been surmised that the present writer maintains the historicity of the patriarchal narratives, although it is impossible to deny the fact that sometimes the material may have been "legendized" just a bit and perhaps heightened as a means of intensifying the dominant characteristics in the patriarch's life. But where heightening has occurred, it is perhaps more valuable than historical fact in that it reveals the soul and pulse of a people who are certain that they live and move under the domination of God. From Skinner's commentary on Genesis, two pertinent suggestions should be remembered:

(1) It is a safe maxim that tradition does not invent names. It would seem that since the names are present, they must have been real names.[6]

---

[5]Cf. Ishmael, 16:11; 17:20; 21:17; Isaac, 17:17; 18:12; 21:9; Jacob, 32:28.
[6]Skinner, *op. cit.*, p. xxxiv.

(2) It is historically credible, as the Scriptures seem to indicate, that there was a divine call summoning a man through whom there was introduced a new era in God's dealing with mankind (cf. Isa. 41:8 f.). Personal experiences verify such a possibility.[7]

Two further quotations from Skinner's commentary on Genesis are helpful at this latter point. The first has to do with the prophetic character of the Abrahamic story.

Nothing in short, forbids us to see in Abraham the first of that long series of prophets through whom God communicated to Israel the knowledge of Himself. Nor is there anything in the religion of Abraham which the mind of an early age could not grasp."[8]

The second has to do with faith.

He [Abraham] moves before us on the page of Scripture as the man through whom faith, the living principle of true religion, became a force in human life. It is difficult to think that so great a conception grew out of nothing. As we read the story, we may well trust the instinct which tells us that here we are face to face with an act of the living God in history, and an act whose significance was never lost in Israelite tradition.[9]

It is important, of course, not to claim too much—that would be just as grievous a sin and error as to suggest no historicity at all. Insofar as the author knows, and as attested by H. H. Rowley, there is not, outside the Bible, a "direct reference in any other source to any incident in the lives of the patriarchs as recorded in the Bible; yet of the credibility of the biblical record we have greater knowledge than was even quite recently available."[10]

In other words, there are a great many evidences which,

---

[7]*Ibid.*, p. xxxvi.
[8]*Ibid.*, p. xxxvii.
[9]*Ibid.*
[10]H. H. Rowley, *The Servant of the Lord and Other Essays on the Old Testament* (London: Lutterworth Press, 1952), p. 272.

while not giving conclusive proof, lend strong credence to the historicity of the patriarchs. The evidences are twofold. They are briefly used here and will be used by way of illustration and explanation as pursuit is made into the individual passages.

The first suggestion is that the patriarchal narratives are in agreement with the general cultural milieu of the life and age which they represent. The life and culture of Canaan as reflected in Genesis has been proved to be substantially that of Canaan from 2000 B.C. and following.[11]

This is true in the area of worship, for it has been fairly well established by the excavations of Woolley at Ur that Ur and Haran were great centers of moon god worship. A similar worship with a temple to the moon god has been found at Mari, which lay on the route from Ur to Haran and about halfway in between.

In the story of the patriarchs are also found "moon" names. The Ras Shamra tablets seem to infer that Terah was used as the name of a moon deity. This was also true of the name Laban, while the names of Sarah and Milcah were also associated with moon worship. Now this does not imply that Terah was a moon god, but it shows harmony with the general cultural milieu of the times. In the home community of the author, there were many boys named Franklin Delano Smith, Jones, etc. It demonstrated the general tenor of the times. Often, the name of the existing deities is reflected in the names of the people of an age. This reflection of the moon worship is a good reflection of the Scriptures, too, for Joshua 24:2 says: "Your fathers dwelt on the other side of the flood in old time, even Terah, the father of Abraham, and the father of Nachor: and they served other gods."

The fact that the names are not fictitious inventions can be seen easily in that these very names were quite common to that age. Some Babylonian letters from modern Delam, a few

---

[11]Hooke, *The Siege Perilous,* p. 148.

miles south of Borsippa, *ca.* 1800 B.C., mention the name Abram. Incorporated, also, is the story of Abram, a small farmer who rented land from a well-to-do farmer. This is not the biblical Abraham, for this man was the son of a certain Amil-Ishtar; but it does show that the name Abraham was a personal name during this period. Names similar to Isaac, Jacob, and Joseph also occur. The name Yakubel (Jacob) occurs some six times in various tablets. There is no doubt that these names were frequent personal names during the early period.

Relative to commerce, a Babylonian chronicle relates that during the reign of Samsuiluna, successor to Hammurabi, a man in Sippar leased a wagon for a year and stated in the contract was the agreement that this wagon could not be driven to Kittim, that is, the coastlands of the Mediterranean. Apparently, travel between the two points must have been fairly heavy if one could not lease a cart without taking into account the possibility that it might be used for such a long journey. Thus, such a trip as recorded for Abraham is not doubtful.

Place names also indicate the same general cultural milieu. In 1905, Breasted in *A History of Egypt* published part of a picture[12] which showed an inscription on the walls of the temple at Karnak on which the biblical Shishak, 945-924 B.C. (cf. 1 Kings 14; 2 Chron. 12), recorded the names of places which he had conquered in Palestine. One place he conquered was known as "the Field of Abram." Now this indicates several things. It indicates that the tradition believed sufficiently in a historical Abram to name territory after him, and, also, it indicates that the Abram of tradition was not an invention of the eighth- or seventh-century prophets or prophetic circles. Place names are often built around the names of individuals. The ancestors of Abraham are reflected in several ancient cities in the Mesopotamian area. Pelug sug-

---

[12]James Henry Breasted, *A History of Egypt* (2d ed.; New York: Charles Scribner's Sons, 1909), p. 536.

gests Paliga at the mouth of the Khabur, while Nahor reflects the city of Nakhur in the region of Haran. Serug corresponds to Sarugi.[13]

Other evidences are of an archaeological nature. Much inscriptional material unearthed by archaeology is of great value in understanding the period. Among such are the Mari tablets from the city of Mari, on the middle Euphrates. From the archives of one of its palaces, over twenty thousand tablets have been recovered. In addition to throwing light on the general background of the patriarchal period beginning about 3000 B.C. and continuing forward, the texts conclusively show that Hammurabi, king of Babylon, was a contemporary of the Assyrian king Shamshi-Adad I. The list of the Assyrian kings contained on the Khorsabad king lists dates Shamshi-Adad *ca.* 1748-1716 B.C. An examination of the intricate relationship between him and Hammurabi thus dates Hammurabi *ca.* 1728-1676. The activities of that period have general correspondence to the time of Abraham.

Additional help comes from the Nuzi tablets. Nuzi was a city east of the Tigris and southeast of Nineveh. Excavation was begun there in 1925 by the American School of Oriental Research, under the direction of Edward Chiera. Work at Nuzi indicated that from about 2000 B.C. it was a center for the Hurrians, the biblical Horites of Genesis 14:6 ff. These picture the social conditions, customs, and business transactions of the times.

Numerous tablets from the twelfth and following Egyptian dynasties, 1989-1776 B.C., reflect the period covered in Genesis. A sample is the *Tale of Sinuhe.* This story tells of a political exile from Egypt who fled to Canaan to live. The coloring of the story portrays the natural products of Canaan and the nature of the life of its inhabitants. The tomb of Khnumhotep II of this period pictures some thirty-seven Semitic people

---

[13]G. Ernest Wright, *Biblical Archaeology* (Philadelphia: Westminster Press, 1957), p. 41.

entering Egypt requesting trade, thus showing to be feasible the historicity of the excursions made into Egypt by the patriarchs in the time of the lean years of famine.

The archaeological work of W. F. Albright aids in the understanding of the genealogical lists of the patriarchal period. In the biblical lists, Moses is separated from Abraham by about five generations. These genealogies, however, seem actually to go back only about two generations before the Exodus and then they are attached to the names of the patriarchs, Abraham, Isaac, and Jacob (cf. 1 Chron. 6; Ex. 6; Ezra 7). But Albright stresses that this should not cause undue disturbance; for Arab tribal genealogies collected by Max von Oppenheim in *Die Beduinen* often omit names in the intervening links, although the founders of important tribes and real contributors to their life and history are always remembered, regardless of missing links.[14] Hebrews probably followed a similar practice.

Although more closely related to geography than to archaeology, the work of Nelson Glueck in the Transjordan area has proved that there was little or almost no sedentary population in the eastern section of Palestine, other than the Jordan Valley and south of Amman, between the twentieth and thirteenth centuries. Texts from Egypt confirm this, indicating that even western Palestine was in something of a tribal stage about 1900 B.C., although it rapidly developed into a city-state system. However, eastern Palestine remained nomadic throughout this period, thus giving opportunity for the early movements as pictured in the book of Genesis.[15]

Perhaps the above material has been of some help in underscoring the historicity of the period. It must, however, be stressed again that false conclusions should be avoided. Quite possibly some of the stories have been heightened and intensified by materials that are not literally historical, for the pur-

---

[14]William Foxwell Albright, *Recent Discoveries in Bible Lands* (New York: Funk & Wagnalls Co., 1936), pp. 76 f.

[15]Albright, *op. cit.*, p. 75.

pose of the Bible is not merely to give a factual account of
events. It is the subjective, theological history of a religious
faith. If stories have been used as a means of underscoring
that faith, it is to be viewed as but another medium of revelation in the economy of God. The thing which historically has
remained unchanged is *that faith.* It (the faith), we must see!
There would have been no faith had there not been some
people to believe and act. These are the patriarchs. Consequently, we are introduced to the first patriarch, the man
about whom S. H. Hooke says, "In Abraham God found a
response of faith which made the patriarch the 'father of all
them that believe' and won for him the title 'Abraham my
friend.' "[16]

The Conversion Call (11:26 to 12:9)

Before being able to understand the marvelous meaning
and outreach of this call and Abraham's relationship to it, it
will be necessary to go back and view the setting from which
Abram came.

11:31. "And they went forth together from Ur of the
Chaldeans to go into the land of Canaan" (RSV). It is perhaps proper to say that today there is little doubt about the
location of Ur, Abraham's homeland, even though recent
journals have discussed the question of a northern location as
over against a southern one.[17] Gordon relies upon two Scripture passages (Isa. 23:13; Gen. 24:4,7) to support his contention of a northern Ur. Isaiah 23:13 speaks of the "land of the
Chaldeans"; and according to Gordon, the context before and
after demands a northern location. In Genesis 24, Abraham
sent his servant back to his homeland to secure a wife for
Isaac; and it would seem that the journey led to Padan-aram,
thus, according to Gordon, meaning that Ur, the homeland,

---

[16]Hooke, *The Siege Perilous,* p. 183.
[17]Cyrus H. Gordon, "Abraham and the Merchants of Ura," *The Journal of
Near Eastern Studies,* XVII (January, 1958), 28-31.

was located there in this northern area of Mesopotamia.[18] For a long time, much tradition seemed to favor a northern location such as that for which Gordon pleads. From pre-Christian times, Ur was located and often placed on maps as the city Urfa, located beyond the Euphrates in northern Syria.

Today that place is of little importance; but during the Middle Ages, known by the name, Edessa, it was a famous capital of Christianity. Visitors there were pointed to a tank of fish, called *Bahr Ibrahim El Halil* (the lake of Abraham the beloved) and located just in front of a Moslem mosque. According to legend associated with the tank, "one day Abraham's cattle were being attacked. When Abraham called upon God for help, fish disguised as armed men jumped from the water, drove off the invaders and then became fish again."[19] This amusing legend is but a sample of the Abrahamic tradition in the area, thus giving some more evidence for belief in a northern location.

However, in 1854 the British Museum sent J. E. Taylor to investigate ruined sites in southern Mesopotamia. One of the ruins which Taylor excavated was *Tell El Mukayyar,* and most today interpret the evidence here as proof that *Tell El Mukayyar* was Abraham's Ur of the Chaldees, located on the western bank of the Euphrates in lower Mesopotamia. In Abraham's day, Ur was apparently much nearer water than it is today; for evidence indicates that the Persian Gulf extended much farther (roughly, some 125 miles) north than it now does. Apparently, the marshy land at the mouth of the gulf was drained and controlled by an intricate system of irrigation ditches. Through their intelligent initiative, the area was made livable, and there Ur was located.[20] According to Woolley, in about 300 B.C., the Euphrates River broke out of its banks,

---

[18]*Ibid.,* p. 31.

[19]Sir Leonard Woolley, *Abraham* (London: Faber & Faber, Ltd., 1936), p. 59.

[20]Today the area is only about fourteen feet above sea level and in Abram's day it was less.

flowed across the open plains, and made a new bed for itself some eleven miles from its former path. The irrigation system thus damaged and the water supply nil, "the surface of the plain was scorched by the tropic sun, the sub-soil was saturated and the constant process of vaporation left in the earth such quantities of salt that today irrigation brings to the surface a white crust like heavy hoar-frost which blights all vegetation at birth."[21] But there Ur was located.

All indications are that Ur was built by Ur-Nammu, the first king of the third dynasty of Ur, in approximately 2270 B.C., and named Ur, perhaps the Semitic form of the Akkadian *Eri* (city). It probably was given this name because it was the most important or chief city in the locality, or, perhaps, because it was there that its once roving inhabitants first settled down. At that time, however, it was not called Ur of the Chaldees. This is an anachronism (a chronological change) which would indicate that the Abrahamic story was written down long after the events occurred. Up until *ca.* 1100 B.C. it was controlled by the Sumerians,[22] but at that time there came into the country a tribe called the Chaldee, who founded a dynasty of kings who thus gave to southern Mesopotamia their own name of Chaldea. It was under the Chaldean (Babylonian) nation of 626 B.C. that the area became extremely significant.

It was a feat just to irrigate the dry land and make it fertile. This alone should indicate that neither Abram nor his people could be characterized by the term "ignoramous" or backward.

Ur, the home of some 250,000 population, was a seat of great civilization. As attested by thousands of recovered clay tablets, its people gave birth to a codification of law, a standard system of weights and measures, and skilled studies in medicine, geometry, and the art of metallurgy. She built great ziggurats—one has been found which dates to Abram's

---

[21]Woolley, *op. cit.*, p. 69.
[22]That entire locale was thus called "Sumer."

time. At its summit was a temple to Nannar, the moon goddess. The temple was built of blue glazed tile, with a kitchen set aside for the proper preparation of sacrifices. Individual chapels to the moon goddess were scattered throughout the city.

Private homes in the narrow streets had chapels, often with bodies buried beneath. Some fifty other deities were also in the pantheon there. Among them were Enlil, god of the storm; Anu, god of the heavens; and Ea, god of the earth and deep. Each family seems to have had its own peculiar family god which stood in relation to the family as Nannar stood in relation to the city of Ur.

Thus, although Abraham's was in many ways an enlightened and cultured environment, it was a pagan one. From such a polytheistic background, reflected scripturally in Joshua 24:2,15, Abraham came.

Suffering, as frequently it does, seems to have served as a quickening of purpose for Terah, Abraham's father; for it was at the death of his son Haran (11:31) that Terah decided to leave this pagan environment.

11:32 f. Actually, little is known about Haran, the place where the call stirred Abram, except that it, too, was a center of moon worship. Very little had been left behind when Abram moved from Ur to Haran, for it afforded a similar environment. The term Haran seems to mean "road," and it probably got such a name because it was a "road city," or junction point, for several trade routes running through the area. An inscription found there speaks of the moon god as the baal (lord) of Haran, showing that the city felt itself to be under the special protection of Nannar. But it is important to remember that it was here that the so-called conversion call of Abram was experienced. Stephen in Acts 7 spoke of the call as having come at Ur of the Chaldees, but apparently he was viewing everything which had happened from an over-all perspective.

The Call in Perspective

Certainly one cannot read the story of the call of Abram without experiencing a realization of some basic principles common to genuine religion. Very evident is the *revelation* of God to man. Something *happened* to Abraham. The recognition of God's sovereignty is an integral part of the call. From the beginning, Abraham seemed to recognize that *God was in control;* and there was something he, Abraham, had to do because God was sovereign. Abraham realized that God had revealed himself; and with this revelation, there was a corresponding demand—the demand that he do something *about* the revelation which he had received. This continues to be a basic principle of religion—that revelation involves demand, privilege involves responsibility.

Perhaps it is well here to be reminded that this call becomes the basis of the covenant between God and Abraham, the covenant to which attention must be given later. Without the call there would have been no covenant, for it is an inherent part of the call.

The phrase "conversion call" has been used, not because Abraham's experience is to be equated to what is meant by the modern use of the term conversion, but because the call involved a price about which Abram had to make a decision. There seems to be intentional pathos in the lingering description of the things he had to leave—thy *land*, thy *kindred*, thy *father's house*. This was no easy task, and he had to decide whether he would or would not accept the call. It was literally "his father's house" that Abram was asked to leave; for when Abram left home, his father was still living. At Abram's birth, Terah was seventy years of age (11:26). Abram departed Haran at the age of seventy-five (12:4), thus, making his father one hundred forty-five years of age. Terah did not die until his two hundred and fifth year (11:32). In other words, there remained to him sixty additional years after Abram set out. It was not an easy thing to depart from the family group; for society—even as in some parts of Nigeria today—was patriarchal, solidified by the family's existence together in something of a family unit, with all of the sons, daughters-in-law, and children gathered around. Abraham would not break accepted practice without a struggle, but he saw the necessity of sacrifice through personal choice and decision, as so often is true in the call from God.

The Elements of the Call

Someone has suggested that in the call were the five basic elements—election, benediction, commission, intention, and condition. Actually, commission and intention are one; so the four—election, benediction, commission, and condition—will be considered.

Election—"Now the Lord said to Abram, 'Go from your country'" (12:1, RSV). There is no possibility of forgetting the matter of election in the call, for it was perhaps the realization of such which "converted" him from his polytheistic background to a better faith. Everywhere in the Old Testament, to be traced originally back to Abram, election simply is assumed. According to R. L. Ottley, "The principle of election is obviously conceived to be a primary element in the Divine method, and accordingly the whole story of Genesis describes the response made to God's action by successive individuals."[23]

As stated previously, to suggest the principle of election is to assume that Abram and the other Old Testament patriarchs understood that God showed himself to, and impressed himself upon, the inner lives of the people. Election is possible only when man has somehow been awakened to a certain susceptibility to the divine self-revelation. The only adequate answer of explanation . . .

---

[23]Robert L. Ottley, *Aspects of the Old Testament* (London and New York: Longmans, Green & Co., Ltd., 1897), p. 118.

of the rise and growth of Hebrew religion is the supposition that God actually made known His will to some individual human spirit, and manifested Himself to him singly and alone. Abraham's history, says Dean Church, is marked as a history of a man, a soul by itself in relation to Almighty God; not as one of a company of a favoured brotherhood, or chosen body, but in all his doings single and alone, alone with the Alone, one with One, with his Maker as he was born—and as he dies, alone: the individual soul, standing all by itself, in the presence of its Author and Sustainer, called by Him and answering to His call, choosing, acting, obeying, from the last depths and secrets of its being.[24]

In other words, it was neither ambition, restlessness, lust of conquest, or greed of gain which led Abram to go; but it was the consciousness of divine presence and the submission to that presence which caused him to go forth. Thus, it has been suggested that his election through revelation was a consciousness that God was asking him to leave his present abode, that he was bidding him to leave it in favor of another, and that although there was some certainty in what he was to do, there was much obscurity hovering over it.

To speak of election through revelation demands some concept of Abram's relationship to, or knowledge of, Yahweh. Both Jews and Mohammedans have pondered the problem for a long time. The Book of Jubilees, chapter 12, trying to imagine Abram's departure from a polytheistic to a more monotheistic faith, tells how "like Gideon he [Abram] burned to the ground the idol temple of his native place . . . and how Haran [brother of Abram; father of Lot] perished in the flames as he tried to rescue the images of the gods whom he still served."[25] It is only a legend but it might have been reality. Other Jewish and Mohammedan traditions picture him as first trying to worship the stars, the moon, and the sun, but they

---

[24]*Ibid.*

[25]William J. Deane, *Abraham: His Life and Times* (London: James Nisbet & Co., Ltd., n.d.), p. 18.

disappeared for half of each day. Therefore, he decided to worship the power behind these bodies. Thus, Abram is pictured as breaking all of the idols except a large life-sized one. The father sought who broke them. "Ask the idol" said Abram, "if he can't speak he isn't worth worshiping." Of course, this is only the speculation of tradition, but it shows the widely persistent belief that Abram had a view of God which contrasted with that ordinarily held in his day.

This is not to say that Abram was a monotheist, but it is to say that he had a concept of God different from that of his pagan neighbors, even though nowhere is there any emphatic inference to the fact that Abram believed that only one God existed. Since the fact of election demanded Abram's response to someone, an excursion at this point to try to ascertain to whom he believed he responded is perfectly in order.

Terah, the father, and perhaps Abram also at one time or another, worshiped idols, i.e., believed in the existence of more than one God (cf. Josh. 24:2,15). But this does not mean that they did not worship Yahweh also. The name Yahweh or Yah occurs as the name of a god in the Babylonian pantheon, thus indicating that it is an ancient name. Though, to be sure, it is in the J document, Laban, like Terah a descendant of Shem, is represented as a Yahweh worshiper (cf. Gen. 24:21, 50-51; 31:53).

Is it not possible that a purer and earlier Yahweh worship had been corrupted because of life in Sumerian surroundings? It has been suggested by Josephus in *Antiquities* I, 6:6, that when Haran died, Terah decided to get his family away from this influence which minimized the importance of Yahweh. Subsequently, the complete story of what advance was made in their knowledge of God does not occur in Genesis. One does know that progress of some kind was made, for Terah is pictured as having had Yahweh as his God. Terah's was not an isolated knowledge, for it is to be remembered that Abraham sent back to get Rebekah for Isaac; for her family had a similar idea of God to his own (Gen. 24). To Abram and his clan, other gods might have existed. Perhaps they attributed to these other gods certain powers, but they were *as nothing* to the supreme. They were to receive no worship, and a god not worshiped actually became no god at all. This was far above the fetishism, or animism, or even the henotheism of the early period. Abram's belief was the higher monolatry, the recognition of a belief in many gods but the supreme domination of, and allegiance to, one God, which really in effect amounts in the mind of the individual to allegiance to, and belief in, only one God.

This seems to be emphasized in the name characteristically ascribed to Abram's god, *El Shaddai,* which seems to mean "God Almighty," the supreme power in heaven and in earth.[26] Notice that it is in emphasizing extremely spiritual matters; peaks of religious experience in the lives of the patriarchs, such as the making of the covenant with Abraham (Gen 17: 1 f.), the Bethel experience in the life of Jacob (Gen. 28:3), the changing of Jacob's name from "deceiver" to "Israel" (Gen. 35:10); and in the important Joseph stories that the term *El Shaddai* is used. This cannot be explained with the suggestion that this simply is the concept of one document, for the term *El Shaddai* occurs in more than one document.[27]

Never again is there any evidence that Abram tried to cling to an old god; for the record contrasts Abram and the leading patriarchs, who never did completely throw off their old allegiances, such as is to be seen in Laban's quest for his teraphim (Gen. 31:19) and in Jacob's lapse from his high ideal which eventually necessitated his "return to Bethel" decision (Gen. 35:2). Thus, Abram, saw and worshiped only one god and tried to lead his successors to do the same. It was by this one supreme God that Abram felt himself to be elected.

---

[26]Cf. Ex. 6:3; Gen. 17:1; 28:3; 35:11; 43:14; 48:3; 49:25.

[27]P—Gen. 17:1; 28:3; 35:11; 48:3; Ex. 6:3; J—Gen. 43:14; 49:25; E—Gen. 35 (Some attribute portions of this chapter to the Priestly source).

If this election of an individual was basic to the initiation of God's answer to man's need, why then did the election fall upon Abram? The answer to the question lies in the realm of supposition. Perhaps God's call to others met with negative response. This is so often the case. Or perhaps there was something in Abram's background which aided in the choice.

Perhaps a man from Ur was needed. Ur was the most cultured city in the world at that time. One who had absorbed the advantages of such a cultured environment would never be tempted to be assimilated into the culture of Palestine. Consciously leaving the stronghold of polytheism, he would know how to meet it in Palestine. Sumerian culture traditionally emphasized individual rights and values such as were needed in the ethical and moral religion of which Abram was a part.

A Semite was needed, for with a better developed understanding of God, he could best pass on the traditions of the creation and the Flood; but, perhaps as much as anything, a man of faith was needed. This was really Abram's only claim to fame. As F. B. Meyer suggested, even as Saul was in the bosom of the Sanhedrin, and as Luther was in the cloister of a pagan church, so Abraham was a man of faith in the midst of corrupt cities.[28]

Why?—there is really no answer except that God in his grace *elected* to do it. This is the only sure answer for anyone's call in any generation. It can never be explained by any merit of man, no matter who that man may be

Benediction.—"And I will bless you . . . I will bless those who bless you" (12:2-3, RSV). This election did involve for Abram a benediction, the second element of the conversion call. Abram went out with a hope and a promise; his was not a blind faith, for there was the statement of blessing and the promise of direction—"to the land that I will show you."

---

[28]F. B. Meyer, *Abraham or, The Obedience of Faith* (London: Morgan & Scott, Ltd., 1911), p. 8.

It is to this element in the call in Abraham's consciousness and in that of the children of Abraham that some historians like Arnold Toynbee have objected. In his book, *An Historian's Approach to Religion,* Toynbee admires the Judaic concept of one true and great God; but he objects to what he calls the Jewish "self-centeredness" in casting themselves in rivalry with, and in ignoring, the rest of mankind in considering themselves to be God's chosen people who, as he says: "in virtue of God's choice of them, have a key part to play in History—in contrast to a heathen majority of Mankind who are worshippers of false gods."[29]

The result he suggests is that the God who is so favored as above all other gods sets up a process of thinking which says that the Chosen People are *better* than other people. He goes on to say that "their abiding belief in their own uniqueness still orients them towards a center that lies in themselves and not in the God from whose fiat their uniqueness derives."[30]

Thus, Toynbee objects to the element of benediction in the call of Abraham and to the doctrine of a chosen people. It is at this point that Toynbee and others, even the Jewish people themselves, lack a comprehension of other elements in the call. The blessing was not an "end-all" but was to accomplish a definite purpose. Failure to realize and to accomplish the purpose meant the withdrawal or abdication of the blessing, as the subsequent history of the Hebrews after Abraham demonstrated.

Commission.—"So that you will be a blessing . . . and by you all the families of the earth will bless themselves" (12:2-3, RSV). The intention expressed through the commission in some way answers the question of why God chose Abraham when the question is asked from a different perspective. This answer is preserved in ancient literature in five places, the

---

[29]Arnold Toynbee, *An Historian's Approach to Religion* (London: Oxford University Press, 1956), p. 12.

[30]*Ibid.,* p. 13.

five being contained in the J and E documents, namely, Genesis 12:3; 18:18; 28:14 in J, and Genesis 22:18; 26:4 in E.

The sum total is that Abram is to demonstrate to the world God's purpose and requirements. The primary emphasis is not that Abraham shall be blessed but that he shall be a blessing. He was to minister to others. Those to whom he ministered and who followed him were to amount to something. This causes Genesis 1-11 to flash back. This commission involves the picking up of Genesis 1-11, showing *how* those caught in the snares of sin can begin to amount to something. To be sure, the Jewish people as a whole forgot this; thus, the punishment of the Exile. To take the blessings for one's self is to miss God's intention.

Note the contrast and change in meaning as rendered according to the Revised Standard Version above and by the King James and American Standard versions which read, "and in thee shall all families of the earth be blessed." Upon looking at the Hebrew, there is no doubt but that the Revised Standard translation is more accurate. The verb for "bless" in the present context is what is known in the Hebrew language as a *niphal*, and it permits either a passive or a reflexive translation. However, when the intention is repeated in the E strata, it uses the Hebrew *hithpael* form which definitely requires a reflexive translation. Apparently, this would necessitate a reflexive translation for this original passage. Thus, the intention of God in the commission becomes clear. It was that the name of Abraham should be a symbol—he and his family and his descendants were to stand for faith. Abraham was to be a symbol of "how blessed folk would be" when they had this kind of faith. The blessings of mankind are dependent upon the quality of faith represented by Abraham. When men possess such faith, they in turn bring blessings to themselves.[31] Abraham was to be the means of the establish-

---

[31]Cf. S. R. Driver, *Sermons on Subjects Connected with the Old Testament* (London: Methuen & Co., 1892), pp. 5 ff.

ment of a community of faith, i. e., to create a redemptive community which would be the medium of overcoming mankind's sin.[32]

Actually, within the New Testament there is a passage which has basic kinship to the purpose of Genesis 12:3. Matthew 16:18 reads, "And I tell you, you are Peter, and on this rock I will build my church, and the powers of death shall not prevail against it." On the kind of faith Peter represented, the kingdom was to be built with all of the blessedness which it involved. This is basically the idea which one finds in the conversion call of Abram. Thus, upon Abram lay the responsibility of fulfilling the intention of God in demonstrating to the men of his day the kind of faith needed to relate one to God. G. Ernest Wright buttresses what has just been said when he writes:

Are we to assume that those who compiled and rewrote these early oral traditions with this view of human history in mind had no answer to the distressing problem which they raised? It is entirely likely that the creation and patriarchal traditions once were circulated independently. But the J writer has brought them together, and following the tower of Babel story we are immediately informed of the election of Abraham. Considering the coherent nature of the J presentation, it is impossible to assume that the two are unrelated. Indeed, the only logical assumption is that the election of Israel in some way must be the answer to the plight of man. Second Isaiah, therefore, is elaborating and deepening no newly invented doctrine when he proclaims:

"Thus saith the God, Yahweh,
   Who created the heavens and stretched them out,
Who spread out the earth and its offspring,
   Who hast given breath to the people upon it,
   And spirit to those who walk on it:
I am Yahweh;
   I have called thee in righteousness;

---

[32]Norman K. Gottwald, *A Light to the Nations* (New York: Harper & Bros., 1959), p. 230.

> I have taken hold of thy hand;
> I have preserved you and given you
> For a covenant of the people,
> For a light to the nations,
> For opening the eyes of the blind,
> For bringing out prisoners from the dungeon,
> From jail those who sit in darkness" (Isa. 42:5-7).[33]

Condition.—Although Genesis 12 does not specifically state such, it implies this element of condition, which apparently Toynbee and others have failed to appreciate in their evaluation of the place of Abraham and the Hebrews. There had to be the response of obedience and faith. These blessings and this use of Abraham were to occur upon the condition that he actually *pulled out from* his homeland. But simply pulling out and giving up the homeland and the family was not enough. Contemporary records from the period show that there was a general trek of the Habiru from Sumeria to Palestine at the time. Many folk had pulled up stakes and left home. Abraham was remembered above the others because of a positive response to God's condition—the response of faith.

This positive attitude with which Abraham responded is mentioned later (Gen. 15:6, RSV), "And he believed the Lord; and he reckoned it to him as righteousness," or more literally, "he *leaned* on God [placed confidence in, gave credit to] and he viewed him as righteous."

That Abram met the condition of confidence in God is demonstrated over and over again; for *nearly* everywhere he pitched his tent, Abram built an altar (cf. 12:7). One can imagine the impressions which he felt as his call was strengthened by his actual arrival in Canaan! The arrival there verified that he had been right in responding with faith. He discovered that when one responds by faith to the condition of

---

[33]Wright, *The Old Testament Against Its Environment*, p. 53.

obedience, he reaches his destination. "When they had come to the land of Canaan, . . . the Lord appeared to Abram, and said, 'To your descendants I will give this land.' So he built there an altar to the Lord" (12:5-7, RSV). Hence, the repeated clarification of this call was strengthened through the erection of altars on the journey.

Abram's initial response to that call was long remembered. Even the first oak tree which shaded his worship (12:6 f.) was venerated as the place of a great expression of confidence in God. Such was remembered in Jacob's day (Gen. 35:1-4). The locale to which he came was Shechem, which lay in a valley sheltered by Gerizim on one side and Ebal on the other.

Perhaps it should be said here that it is not possible to ascertain exactly where that journey of faith led Abraham. The record is meager, although there are some traditions. Josephus in *Antiquities* I, 7:2 states that Abram left Haran and went to Damascus, where he reigned for a while as king but that eventually he was compelled by an uprising of the people to depart into Canaan. That there may be some truth in the tradition of a time spent in Damascus is made possible in that a village still remains today, located about a mile and a half from the northern gate of Damascus, called "Abram's Dwelling." Justin also makes reference to the same tradition. Support of additional nature is to be found in that Abram had as his steward, Eliezer of Damascus (15:2), or as the Hebrew literally reads, *Damasek Eliezer,* much in the same sense that one would speak of the "Kansas City Smiths" or the "Louisville Nortons." But if he ever lived in Damascus, it was not to tarry long.

He seems to have arrived in Canaan less than a year after his departure from Haran. The call to which he responded thus led him to Canaan, the crossroads of the world, a country capable of producing foodstuff, a country capable of providing natural protection for a people to be builded who could give God's answer to man's needs in a needy world.

The Call Forgotten (12:10-20; 20:1-18; 26:1-16)

The Trying Ordeal

It is difficult to fathom how one who had learned so much could forget so quickly, but Abram did. Two severe tests early tried Abram's faith. Circumstances seemed to be against him, for when he arrived in Canaan, the land was already occupied ("the Canaanites were in the land," 12:6). Furthermore, he seemed to be faced with a great contradiction. He expected blessing; but shortly after reaching Canaan, he was faced with a severe famine (12:10 f.). This is so often true. One arrives at what he thinks his goal to be and troubles come to test his faith, rousing him from the ease which he expected and desired. New Christians often have this experience. Apparently, Abram's faith had not anticipated the thorns, for his faith seems to have faltered.

Abram failed to ask God what to do in the crisis of famine and instead went straight to Egypt. His lack of faith was in turn followed by a lack of worship, for there was no effort to build an altar in Egypt. Having been guilty of falsehood in giving his wife to Pharaoh, he in turn was faced with loss of opportunity. His opportunity to fulfil his covenant witness and responsibility was killed by his lack of integrity.

To be certain, Abram learned from the experience the lesson that his God was a God of truth (12:17). How horrible that a heathen king had to teach it to him by accusing him of lying. He learned that life could not be lived by his own ingenuity and, finally, that he had to pay for his sin. Pharaoh gave Abram maid-servants, man-servants, she-asses, oxen, and camels. Abram got wealth, but he lived to regret the day that he accepted a certain maid-servant named Hagar. One does not escape his sins. Even the saint pays the consequences. Thus, in the call of Abraham, one can see various implications which are involved in the relationship of a people to God through faith.

A Historical Problem

Earlier much effort was expended for the purpose of maintaining the historicity of the patriarchal narratives. However, this is not to deny such historical problems as are met in this particular section, Genesis 12:10 f.—those which need to be faced at this juncture. To get the picture in perspective, chapter 20 and chapter 26:1-16 must be compared with chapter 12:10 f.

12:10-20 (J source). Abram traveled *toward* Egypt[34] because there was a famine in the land of Palestine. Now this may mean simply that he traveled south, possibly stopping at the Negeb region.

A second element in the report of chapter 12 is that since Sarai was so beautiful, Abram feared that some Egyptian would be captivated by her beauty and slay him, the husband, in order to have Sarai as his very own. Thus, Abram urged Sarai to falsify the situation and claim to be his sister, which apparently she was quite willing to do. In passing, though it has no direct connection with the problem at hand, it is interesting to note that this tradition of Sarai's beauty persisted in Hebrew tradition. Dr. Yigael Yadin, professor of archaeology at the Hebrew University in Jerusalem calls attention to her beauty as described in one of the Dead Sea Scrolls which was found in 1947. This account is supposedly based on that of one Karkanos, an Egyptian minister of the sixteenth century B.C., who said:

How . . . beautiful the look of her face . . . and how fine is the hair of her head, how pleasing her nose and all the radiance of her face. . . . How beautiful her breast and how lovely all her whiteness.

Her arms are goodly to look upon and her hands, how perfect . . . all the appearances of her hands.

Her legs how beautiful and how without blemish her thighs.

---

[34]This is the proper translation of the *he directive* on the word Egypt in verse 10.

All the maidens and all the bridges that go beneath the wedding canopy are not more fair than she. And above all women is she lovely and higher in beauty than much wisdom in her, and the tip of her hands is comely.[35]

The Egyptians did think that she was beautiful, so she was taken into Pharaoh's house. Abram prospered, but Pharaoh and his house suffered plagues. Upon learning the truth about Sarai, Pharaoh sent Sarai and Abram from the land so as to stop the displeasure of Abram's God.

20:1-18 (E source). Now notice the similarities in this account. Abraham journeyed to the south toward the Negeb region, but this time he dwelled at Gerar, over which Abimelech was king, a place located between Kadesh and Shur. Abraham spoke falsely about his relationship with Sarah, and Abimelech, thinking that Sarah was Abram's sister, took her. Through a dream, Abimelech learned the truth about the identity of Sarah, and disaster did not abate until Abraham took his wife and departed.

26:1-16 (J source?). Similar characteristics are presented again. There was a famine in the land, although it is stated that this was "besides the former famine that was in the days of Abraham." Isaac went to Gerar, where lived Abimelech, the same name as is used in chapter 20. Isaac presented Rebekah as his sister, for she was a beautiful woman; and he feared lest someone kill him to take Rebekah as wife. Abimelech discovered Isaac fondling Rebekah and realized that she was Isaac's wife and not his sister. Isaac then got his wife back, prospered, and found it necessary to leave the country.

Now it is entirely possible that these should be considered three different stories as depicted. However, one must notice that in chapter 20 it is Abraham who deals with Abimelech at Gerar, whereas in chapter 26 it is Isaac who deals with

---

[35]*Courier-Journal* (Louisville), November 14, 1957.

Abimelech of Gerar. This is to say nothing of the twofold and dismal failure to learn a lesson from the past.

The present writer would suggest that actually the three passages deal with only two different occasions. Both chapters 12 and 20 refer to the same, that is, one event in the life of Abraham. The differences noted are not many. In both cases the relationship is that between Abraham and Sarah; the story is essentially the same, although there is the difference of the first dealing with the Pharaoh and the second with Abimelech. But this might be accounted for by two possibilities. The locality in which Gerar was situated may have been under the control of Egypt, with Abimelech acting in behalf of the Pharaoh. However, it must be noted that Gerar is distant from the Egyptian capital of that day, for both in the Middle Kingdom (1989-1776) and in the Second Intermediate Period (1776-1570) the capital was located at Memphis, some 250 miles away. A better suggestion is the acknowledgment that one is dealing with two sources, J and E, and that the years saw variations in the traditions. The problem of Gerar's being in the hands of the Philistines may be explained as an anachronism, such as that in Genesis 21:32.

Chapter 26 appears to be a second happening. Isaac, in some ways characteristically weak, simply got into trouble by the same method as did Abraham. Perhaps testimony to the weakness of Isaac is to be seen in that, except for the expression "Abraham, Isaac, and Jacob," Isaac is mentioned only two other times in the Old Testament (Amos 7:9,16). This suggestion is made even though Skinner disagrees, arguing with a feeble case, that chapter 26 is simply a misplaced appendix to the Abrahamic narrative.[36]

If one cannot be certain of the facts of historicity, what is to be received from the stories? The basic core of the stories is the representation of *what happens when a man fails to use*

---

[36]Skinner, *op. cit.*, p. 355.

his faith. The differences in detail do not affect this main and central truth. Through the stories various lessons are learned, such as God's providence for his own, for he protected Abram; the sinful nature of even the best of men; the social effects of sin; the universal sovereignty of God, both within and outside of Israel; the sanctity of the institution of marriage (20:3); and the validity of intercessory prayer (20:17). For the illustration of such themes as these the stories were recorded.

Choice and Its Results (13-14)

The setting for this particular section transpires initially in the Bethel-Hai region, to the northwest of the Dead Sea. It was to this place that Abram went upon his return from Egypt. It was for Abram a place of recommitment and rededication after his lapse in Egypt (13:3). Bethel was a sacred locale for him. There (12:8) initially he had set up an altar, and he establishes it again. He calls once more upon the name of the covenant God, the same God who had first called him.

It was apparently just after this recommitment that the episode with Lot occurred. There are many periods of testing in Abraham's life, and this one, coming as it did just after his recommitment, is to ascertain whether he has really shaken off the lapse and weakness which had seized him in Egypt.

Characters Involved

The necessity for the choice is suggested in verse 6; prosperity of cattle and possessions intensified the necessity of larger pasture land. It is amazing how then, as so often now, the material brought strife. Apparently, the Genesis compiler had that particular emphasis in mind. This kind of sin in man has been stressed by the author before in the tower of Babel setting, with its desire for a great material civilization, and will be stressed again in the deception of material things in the Jacob-Esau narratives, the Jacob-Laban stories, and in the strife between the herdsmen of Isaac and the Philistines.

Thus, the comprehension of the blessing pertinent to the situation is simplified through the knowledge of Lot's character, as revealed in his choice. The words are few but the meaning is clear, "Lot chose for himself" (13:11, RSV). It was a choice made without God's advice. The road had begun together, but, apparently, Abram and Lot never really had been together. Abram had set the pace and Lot followed. As someone has suggested, Lot had been one of those men who take right steps, not because they are prompted by obedience to God, but because their friends are taking them. Lot was under the protection and spell of heroic faith, not his own but Abraham's. Another has suggested that Lot was simply a "chip on the bosom of a mighty current" who was looking for the "main chance." He would be righteous until something came along which more immediately seemed profitable. No doubt he saw certain dangers in his choice; but, after all, "business is business," and a man had to look out for himself, so he made the choice. Judging from Lot's reaction, the process of rationalization to cover one's sins is not a modern innovation. Lot was much like the literary character who was religious but about whom the devil was not too concerned, for he knew the man to be only partially religious.[37] Now it is true that 2 Peter 2:7 f., as it looks back on the over-all career of Lot, calls him a "righteous man." The word *dikaion* means *one who is such as he ought to be—upright, virtuous, keeping the commands of God.* Lot was this kind of fellow only so long as it did not cost him too much. He believed in a righteous life, but he was not willing to pay the cost.

On the other hand, the magnanimity of Abram as a man of God was also indicated in the episode. Abram could have reacted in several possible ways. Remembering all that had been promised to him in the initial call experience, he could have said in typical human fashion, "Get out; this all belongs

---

[37] Cf. the delightful book by C. S. Lewis, *The Screwtape Letters* (London: Geoffrey Bles, Ltd., 1942).

to me." Or he could have pointed to a barren strip of land and said, "I'll give you this little piece of land; live on it and be grateful for it." But instead, Abram in effect said, "Take what you want and I'll take what is left." This certainly revealed the greatness of Abram. His recommitment had *taken*, for such magnanimity springs only from fellowship with God. In fact, Lot perhaps realized that Abram would react this way, so he made his choice with some assurance that Abram's unselfishness could be manipulated to his own advantage. At any rate, one sees here something of the spirit of sacrifice which was later to be developed in the Genesis 22 Abraham-Isaac experience. It was the man sensitive to God's will who made the proposal to settle strife. Already Abram was being used in the fulfilment of covenant witness.

Lot's Part

Although a little tedious, later developments can be better understood if a digression is made here as to the location of that which Lot chose. It seemed to be a portion of land not even in Canaan proper (13:12-13), but land to the south and east of the Dead Sea, that which came to be known as Moab. Moab, after whom the country was named, according to Genesis 19:37, was a son of Lot. At least tradition associates Lot with Moab. It seemed to be in a setting occupied by a rough element (13:13). It was a choice which brought Lot a great estate but bad neighbors. In this emphasis, the writer carefully and skilfully is laying the groundwork for what is to follow in chapters 14, 18, and 19.

Most agree today that the actual cities near which Lot chose to make his residence were in the valley of the Jordan in the mountainous Dead Sea area at its southern extremity. Although the translations speak of Lot's choice as including all of the Jordan "valley," the word used is the Hebrew *kikar*, which means a "round" district, such as the basin area at the lower end of the Dead Sea.

Evidence from chapter 14 also indicates that the location was south, for it was from thence that they pursued the retreating kings in a northerly direction. From 14:10, one learns that this was an area full of slime pits, or as it is often translated, "bitumin pits." The word is *chemar*, that stuff used for mortar in the building of the tower of Babel (11:3) and as waterproofing material for the ark in which Moses was placed. This material has been found in large measures, especially at the southern part of the Dead Sea, where it oozes from rocks from within and outside the sea. It is particularly noticeable at the time of earthquakes.

Furthermore, when Sodom was destroyed (19:28), Abram, on the morning after the catastrophe, looked toward Sodom and Gomorrah and saw the smoke of the land going up. If such could be seen by Abram who was living at Hebron, then it must have been a southern rather than a northern direction.

According to 13:10, it was a well-watered area. Although nothing can live in the Dead Sea itself, Albright and Glueck report that even today there are fertile fields and orchards in the southeast corner of the valley.[38] Indications are that the land was even more fertile when attention was given to irrigation. Refreshing fertility comes from three streams pouring down from the mountains of Moab. In 14:3, the section is called "the valley of Siddim (that is, the Salt Sea)." This would suggest that at the time of the writing of the account, the area was already submerged under the Dead Sea. There is evidence that the Dead Sea has been rising in water level and expanding. Islands which in the late 1800's were visible could be traveled over with motorboat in the early 1900's. Comments from external writers[39] and evidence from geology all support this southern location as the starting place for the land which Lot chose.

---

[38] Nelson Glueck, *The River Jordan* (Philadelphia: Westminster Press, 1946), pp. 71-73.
[39] Such as Deodoros, Strabo, Josephus, and Tacitus.

Contrasted Ends

Beginning with chapter 14, the remainder of the chapters in the Abrahamic section seem to develop the theme of a contrast between Lot's bad fortune and Abraham's good fortune, resulting from the choices. One simply cannot read the biblical record without seeing there the representation of the swift fall of the disobedient. The picture of the swift descent of Lot further underscores man's need for redemption. Meyer summarized it this way:

> first he saw; then he chose;
> then he separated himself from Abraham;
>   then he journeyed east;
> then he pitched his tent toward Sodom;
>   then he dwelt there;
> then he became an alderman of the place,
>   and sat in the gate.
> His daughters married two of the men of Sodom;
>   and they probably ranked among the most genteel
> and influential families of the neighborhood.[40]

Chapters 14, 18, and 19, thus picture Lot, while the remainder of the material majors on Abraham although, of course, because of Lot's misfortune, Abram is involved in it all. A look must be taken now at chapter 14.

Conflict with the kings.—Represented as a direct result of his choice is Lot's capture by four eastern kings. This capture took place when four eastern kings made an excursion into Palestine to subdue the rebellion of five minor kings of south Palestine. Upon his capture, Abram rushed to Lot's rescue.

In fairness to all, it should be admitted that here is one of the most difficult passages in all of the Pentateuch. It has so many problems about it that Pfeiffer [41] has made a different

---

[40]Meyer, *op. cit.*, p. 52.
[41]Robert H. Pfeiffer, *Introduction to the Old Testament* (New York: Harper & Bros., 1948), pp. 159-167.

source out of it, S, as have others, such as Eissfeldt with his L source. Based upon outdated information, C. A. Simpson said of this chapter in *The Interpreter's Bible* that the "tale provides evidence of its unhistorical character."[42] Yet, in spite of all of the above, voices such as those of H. H. Rowley, S. H. Hooke, and Nelson Glueck must be heard on the matter.

Material in chapter 14, with all of its problems, still bears testimony that Genesis can no longer be considered as unhistorical in view of the many confirmations of details which recent finds have made available.[43] For instance, Genesis 14:15 used to be regarded as an unsuitable travel route for such an early age, but today we know that there was a route along the Syrian Desert in the early Middle Bronze Age and that the route was periodically spaced with fortresses. This of course does not mean that one can pinpoint all of the characters involved in the chapter or that he can date specifically the material and battle at a certain time, but it does mean that there is no reason to doubt that Abraham was in such an encounter because of the sins of his nephew Lot.

Involved in the understanding of the content of the chapter is an effort to approximate the date of Abraham. Formerly, there seemed to be a foolproof scheme for his date. In 1 Kings 6:1 it is reported that Solomon began to build the Temple in the fourth year of his reign (*ca.* 965), which was 480 years after the Exodus. Adding the two together, the resultant exodus date is roughly 1445 B.C. According to Exodus 12:40, the Hebrews had been in Egypt 430 years, making *ca.* 1874 the time for their entrance into Egypt. Several passages in Genesis (12:4; 21:5; 25:20; 47:9) give us the years of the patriarchs from the departure from Haran by Abram to the entry into Egypt. The total was 215 years, which, when added to 1875, gives *ca.* 2100 B.C. as a date for Abraham. Ability to

---

[42]Simpson, *op. cit.,* p. 590.

[43]Cf. the appropriate sections in H. H. Rowley, *The Servant of the Lord and Other Essays;* S. H. Hooke, *In the Beginning;* Nelson Glueck, *The River Jordan.*

identify the kings in chapter 14 would help to either confirm or cast doubt upon the 2100 B.C. date.

The first king was Amraphel, king of Shinar. Linguistically, some think it possible to equate Amraphel as perhaps a later form of the name Hammurabi. This identification has been acccepted for years, since Shinar is another name for Babylon and since Hammurabi was king of Babylon. Names of authorities can be lined up pro and con about the identification. Voegelin, Albright, Rowley, and Böhl seem tentatively to accept such an identification. Skinner, C. A. Simpson, T. J. Meek, and S. H. Hooke have never accepted this identification.

From evidence found at Mari and elsewhere, Hammurabi should be dated about 1728-1676 or generally around 1700. Just on a chronological basis, this would seem to rule out any identification of Hammurabi and Amraphel, since Abraham's date is 2100 B.C. according to biblical chronology. However, the matter does not end here, for there are other Scripture passages which will not allow such an ancient date for Abraham. The Samaritan Pentateuch and the Septuagint add the phrase "and in the land of Canaan" to Exodus 12:40. Perhaps this was originally true of the Hebrew text. If so, the 430 years would cover not only the sojourn in Egypt but the entire period from Abraham's migration from Haran up to, and including, the Exodus. Paul seems to have so taken it in Galatians 3:17. He must have felt the Septuagint reading to be more accurate. Numerous Old Testament passages interpret or understand the 430 years to cover both the time in Canaan and the sojourn in Egypt (Gen. 15:16; 46:11; Num. 26:57-59; Ex. 6:16-20; Josh. 7:1; Ruth 4:18,22).[44] Thus, the date for Abraham probably ought to be reduced by some 205 years and maybe more. Thus, chronologically, it would be possible to equate Amraphel and Hammurabi.

---

[44] In these passages which mention "generations," it is to be remembered that a generation in the Old Testament is usually considered to be about forty years.

A second king in the story is Arioch, of Ellasar. Ellasar seems to be the Hebrew form of the town of Larsa, one of the important communities of southern Babylonia located on the eastern bank of the Euphrates, a little to the southeast of Warka. Arioch sounds a little like Arriwuk, son of Zeinridin, of the eighteenth century.

Also in the account is the name of Chedorlaomer, king of Elam. Elam lay to the east of Babylonia and included what is now known as Persia. The Elamites began their rule in Mesoptomania *ca.* 1960-1830 and continued through the years until the twelfth century. Babylonian inscriptions indicate that the Elamites sometimes ruled as far as the Mediterranean. It is possible to equate approximately the name Chedorlaomer with one of two Elamite names, either Kuter-Nahhunte or Kuder Lagamor. According to W. F. Albright, the name should be equated to Kuter-Nahhunte of the seventeenth century, while H. P. Scheil, the Assyriologist, equates it with Kuder Lagamor, a name which Scheil claims to have read on the tablets of Hammurabi. If this can be verified, then there are possibly two kings of Genesis 14 equated within the same period.

The last king of the group was Tidal, king of Goiim. Goiim may be a variant spelling of Gutium, an ancient state lying between Babylonia and Media, actually north of Babylonia and stretching to the mountains of Kurdistan. The name Tidal has most often been equated with Tudalia, a Hittite king who ruled this area *ca.* 1720-1680.

Thus, it can be seen from the discussion above that even if the specific identifications which have been attempted cannot be made, at least Abraham and Genesis 14 definitely can be placed within the realm of history. Perhaps the evidence of chapter 14 would indicate even that Abraham definitely should be dated to the period around 1800-1700 B.C.

Even if the identifications made above are not entirely accurate, at least these anti-Canaanite kings are representative of the four main bodies of people ruling at the time of Hammurabi, that is, of the Elamites, Babylonians, Mittanians, and the Hittites. Thus, the first mention of war in the Bible has a historical setting. But far more important, it points out the imperative nature of God's call to Abraham to establish a community of redemptive faith.

By this time Abram had gained enough status among the citizens of the ancient world, at least in his own locale, to be called "the Hebrew" (14:13), the first occurrence of the term in the Old Testament. Although the term has certain religious associations, it also seems to relate Abram to the folk called "Habiru," a people frequently mentioned in the records of the Fertile Crescent and Asia Minor, and variously described as wanderers, slaves, and mercenaries.

In order to save Lot (here called Abram's "brother" rather than "nephew," 14:14, an indication that the term "brother" in the Old Testament is loosely used to mean "kinsman"), Abram seems to have joined his 318 men with many other forces (14:13-14,17).[45] However, Abram gained the center of the stage in the Genesis account, partly because of his ability and partly because he and his people are of most importance in building the story of God's providence in redemption.

The fact that such a small number of fighting men went against the invaders is not alarming. Traveling as far from home as the invaders were, their army and caravan naturally would have been limited in size and only representative of the larger forces at their rulers' command. In addition, it must be remembered that they did not need huge armies for, supposedly, they were not attacking well-organized states or na-

---

[45]Cf. the comment of Glueck: "I believe the figure of 318 to be exactly correct, although aware of the fact that it had to be repeated from father to son for well over a thousand years before there was any possibility of committing it to paper. To this very day there are old men in the tents of Arabia who can recite the history of their ancestors for forty generations, and if in their recital they stray but a jot from the facts, others within hearing will immediately correct them, or supply forgotten details." *Op. cit.*, p. 74.

tions but small individual clans of peoples gathered around
individual localities.

The narrative purposefully is used by the author to continue
the contrast between the characters of Lot and Abraham. Note
the swiftness (14:14) with which Abram was ready to strike;
he was willing and ready within minutes after the tidings from
the valley. He did not delay action. This denotes something
of his forgiveness and compassion for Lot. No bitterness was
held because of the decision which Lot had previously made.

Something of Abram's general ability as a leader is presented
also. He acted with decisiveness, and his people seemed to
be quick to follow with no questioning of his command. At
his voice they were ready to risk their lives to rescue Lot and
the herdsmen of Lot, who formerly had striven with them.

The story also depicts something of Abram's attitude toward
the injustice of the world and his proper attitude in victory;
for regardless of how his experience with Melchizedek is explained, Abram was humbled to worship and was not lifted to
haughtiness by his victory.

Contact with Melchizedek.—The battle over, Abram was
traveling back home and passed through a place called Salem
where there was a priest and ruler of the city named Melchizedek. He came out, met Abram and said that *El Elyon*
(God Most High), the possessor of heaven and earth, had
given Abram victory. To Melchizedek, Abram gave a tenth
of the captured possessions. Subsequently, the king of Sodom
arrived and suggested that Abram should keep all of the goods,
whereupon Abram replied that he had lifted up his hand to
Yahweh, God Most High (*El Elyon*), that he would not take
anything.

Formerly, scholars dismissed this episode as a late interpolation because it was assumed that there was no high priest in
Salem (Jerusalem) in the first half of the second millennium
B.C. It was considered to be anachronistic. However, as in so
many other areas where false judgments have been made,

doubt has been removed by the certainty of facts from archaeo-logical finds. The material from ancient Ras Shamra, along the Phoenician coast, verifies the fact that Canaanite cities did have high priests. There is reason to believe that Salem, identified as the later city of Jerusalem in Psalm 76:2, also had a high priest.

In 1934, George W. Barton uncovered a liturgy incorporated in material at Ras Shamra, a liturgy which seems to have been used for a spring festival at Jerusalem (ca. 1800-1600, the gen-eral period for Abraham and Melchizedek. The city for which the liturgy was in use is called Salem, the same as here, mean-ing of course that Salem (Jerusalem) was an early place of worship. In the text which Barton found, the God worshiped at Salem is called *El*, and in Poem II of the text he is referred to as *gnyt* (possessor-owner) of the gods, the same word used of *El Elyon* in Genesis 14. Certainly Genesis 14 is of a histori-cal core.

To understand Melchizedek's relationship to this liturgy, it is necessary to remember that in prehistoric days, tribes and cities were ruled by kings who probably enjoyed a sacred character.[46]

To relate the story and the background is one thing but to interpret it is another. Various efforts have been made, and one must consider the different possibilities.

(1) Etiological—a later addition by a postexilic editor to show the antiquity of Jerusalem as a center of worship.

Thus, Melchizedek in Jerusalem is a manufactured setting which brings together the ideals of a holy people and a holy city for the first time. The purpose of the fabrication was to intensify Jerusalem's cause by giving her an ancient and im-portant lineage, thus generating larger respect for Zion among the people. However, this can hardly be the case, for the materials with which we are working have too many charac-

---

[46]Even Saul in a later period enjoyed protection because he was a "sacred" person—1 Sam. 24:10.

teristics of history. There are numerous evidences that *Elyon* was an early name for a deity worshiped in numerous locales.[47]

(2) Traditional—an acknowledgment of monotheism to Melchizedek, Abram's superior.

In spite of the fact that there is no evidence that Melchizedek was a Yahweh worshiper, many feel that Melchizedek and Abram did worship the same god. It was for this reason that Abraham gave him his offering. It was a way of acknowledging the victory with thanksgiving to the god who had made victory possible. Thus, since he worshiped through Melchizedek, Abram was recognizing Melchizedek as spiritually his superior. But this hardly seems a proper interpretation when it is remembered that every effort is made throughout this section to build Abram as a superior man of faith, the symbol of redemption. Various other times, as can be seen in chapters 12, 13, and 22, Abram is represented as worshiping, and no priest is needed. Later, when Jacob, at Bethel, made the vow of the tithe, no priest was needed. After all, it is Abraham, through whom God chose to work out his answer to man's need, not Melchizedek.

(3) A declaration of faith.

The author must confess to having been influenced greatly at this point by Eric Voegelin, but the evidence is striking. Apparently, Abram first went to Melchizedek, a comrade who had joined him in battle, to divide some of the spoils. That some religious understanding was involved did not appear until Melchizedek introduced it.

El Elyon means "highest God." In the Ras Shamra texts Baal is referred to as the *Al'iyan* (highest god), and he is also called the "possessor of all things," a phrase used here in verse 19. This recognizes Baal as the supreme deity in the Canaanite pantheon. It would appear, then, that in verse 19, Melchizedek was blessing Abram by the Baal, whom Melchizedek

---

[47]Cf. Num. 24:16; Deut. 32:8; Psalm 7:17; 18:24; 47:2; 57:2.

considered to be the highest god of the city state at Salem. Thus, Melchizedek was extending blessings for, and receiving, tithes in behalf of his *El Elyon,* to be equated with Baal. Out of courtesy, Abram did not object to giving Melchizedek and his god what Melchizedek deemed to be his share of the booty, but that was as far as he was willing to go. When the king of Sodom (v. 21) offered to share the loot with Abram, his conscience was suddenly striken that this could be interpreted as belief in Baal, *El Elyon,* as the giver of victory. Thus, with his soul burdened by his loyalty to Yahweh, Abram halted and rejected the offer in fairly violent and rude language and literally says (vv. 22-23):

> I raise my hand[48] to *Yahweh, El Elyon* the *koneh*
> (owner, possessor, maker) of heavens and earth:
> If from a thread to a shoe-lace, if I take aught
> that is yours. . .
> You shall not say "I have made Abram rich".
> Not for me—
> Only what the young men have eaten, and the portion
> of men who went with me,
> Aner, Eshcol, Mamre,
> Let them take their portion.

This was a dramatic speech, a dangerous burst of his faith into the midst of a loyal Baal setting. He was saying that he would take nothing lest it be thought an acknowledgment of Baal as bestower of victory and as *El Elyon.* The true *Elyon* was Yahweh. Let the men have something if they desired, for they were Baal worshipers, but not so for Abram. Voegelin's words speak with clarity:

It is a dramatic speech; an outburst, holding back on the verge of a betrayal, lapsing into silences to cover what already has been half said. It reveals more than the resentment of a proud nomad

---

[48]This is the gesture which usually accompanies an oath (Cf. Ex. 6:8; Num. 14:30; Deut. 32:40; Ezek. 20:23; Dan. 12:7).

of being made rich by the generosity of a king—if this feeling plays an important role at all. For behind the overt rejection of the King's offer there lies the rejection of Melchizedek and his El Elyon. When Abram raises his hand to Yahweh, he pointedly arrogates the Baal's epithet for his own God. By Yahweh he swears his unfinished oath not to take anything of the King's possession. His professed unwillingness to be made rich by the King, is in reality an indignant refusal to be made rich by the King's Baal. Yahweh is the god who delivers enemies into Abram's hands, not the god of Melchizedek; Yahweh blesses Abram, not the Baal of Jerusalem. . . .[49]

So again there is the contrast between the fall of Lot and the faithfulness of Abram. The one had trouble and the other, to be viewed in succeeding chapters, was the recipient of blessing.

Covenant: Reward to a Man of Faith (15; 17-19)

Chapters 15, 17

Introduction.—Whereas the choice which Lot made involved him in much difficulty, part of which must be viewed again in chapters 18 and 19, Abram's choice was the decision of crucial significance which ultimately led to much blessing. The highlight of the blessing is the covenant of chapters 15 and 17, a reward to this man of faith. But more must come later about the consideration together of these two chapters.

The chronological heading "After these things" introduces the fifteenth chapter. It is difficult to decide just "what things." The phrase might refer to the events of chapter 14. Thus, "after these things" makes reference to the events following the brave action of Abram in defending Lot, and his concluding declaration of faith. This is certainly a long while after his return from Egypt, for Ishmael not only has been born (16:15) but is now approximately thirteen years of age (17:25). One of the greatest difficulties here is that chapter

---

[49]Voegelin, *op. cit.*, p. 192.

14 seems to be from a stratum or document different from that of the material immediately following. This is not serious, however, for it may have been the only stratum actually maintaining a good account on this point. Perhaps this is a development which continues the theme of Abram's magnanimous choice. A blessing and a covenant "spell out" the result of his choice. Chapter 14 provided an interlude to indicate what happened to Lot as a result of his choice, while chapters 15 and following speak of the plight of Abraham in the years following the choice. There is then a contrast between the "plight of Lot," chapter 14, and the "plight of Abraham," chapter 15,

Within chapters 15 and 17, there is a certain anxiety, moodiness, and even fear on the part of Abraham. One can almost feel it as he says hopelessly in 15:2, "O Lord God, what wilt thou give me, for I continue childless." But it is possible to understand this despair when one realizes that as yet Abram had no full-blooded Semitic descendants. This in itself is something of a shame for a Hebrew. It represents a certain failure on the part of the marriage relationship and, of course, a certain failure in the covenant relationship. There was an obligation not only to "be fruitful and multiply and replenish the earth" but also to produce someone who could serve as a means of perpetuating the covenant.

In addition, there must have been a certain physical strain. The war over, he now realized how tired he actually was. Low physical status often leads to emotional and spiritual depression. This was a natural reaction in the quiet after the storm.

Coupled with all of this there was, perhaps, also a feeling of the lack of security in a strange land. That declaration of his faith in chapter 14 was strong enough to alienate many who might have befriended him. It was a clash of religions. The Canaanites attributed their well-being to the majesty and fertility of their god; thus, it is easy to suspect that they were not pleased with Abram's belittlement of their god. Abram realized here that he was an outsider and that he might be in serious trouble. Those very ones, whom only recently he had helped, might turn against him.

His actions in response to the king of Sodom might be the cause of his losing the land he had come to settle. Had he acted too hastily or spoken too quickly?

God in his providence was mindful of Abram's needs, and he answered Abram's dilemma in an appearance which resulted in a double-edged promise. "The word of the Lord came" (הָיָה דְבַר־יְהֹוָה, 15:1) is a constant formula in the prophets for a dynamic appearance of God to the prophet. The phrase is used here in this fashion. Abram is even called a prophet in Genesis 20:7.

Relative to Abram's fear of the physical, God promised to be his protector.[50] As to Abram's childlessness, God promised a perpetuator of the covenant. Although Abram might have "interpreted God's delay as denial," God had not forgotten. There was evident satisfaction in the answer, for Abram "believed the Lord" (15:6). This belief was in spite of seemingly strong improbabilities of bringing to pass some of the things promised. In passing, this would indicate that in the Old Testament there was more than legalism; the inner attitude was important. Of course, that answer was in turn bound and sealed by the covenant.

Covenant passages.—Before the elements of the covenant can be expounded, it will be necessary to make an excursion into the examination of the relationship which the two covenant chapters (15,17) have to each other. To the question there are two possible answers. Some suggest that chapter 15 contains an account of the *initiation* of the covenant, while chapter 17 reports the *renewal* of the covenant. It seems more probable that chapters 15 and 17 are two renderings, for the sake of emphasis, of the same covenant. Looking at the ele-

---

[50]"Fear not, I am your shield."

ments of the covenant in each of the chapters may help to decide.

First, notice the elements as viewed in chapter 15. The promise of an heir is found in verses 1-6. Abram had complained that he would have no son and that in accordance with accepted custom, he would have to name Eliezer as his adopted son. The Nuzi tablets from the Near East serve as external verification that such a practice was common. Those who had no child would adopt someone as son. The adopted son was obligated to care for his foster parents and to give them an honorable burial. In return, the adopted received the inheritance and carried on the family's tradition and tasks. God promised that a genuine son would be the heir.

The promise of a land is found in verses 12b-16.

The covenant ritual is given in verses 7-12a and 17-18a. This is a ceremony in reply to Abram's request for some indication or sign whereby he could know that God would keep his promise. A three-year-old heifer, a she goat, ram, dove, and a pigeon are all to be taken and slit, and the halves are laid opposite each other. A smoking fire pot and a flaming torch pass between these pieces (cf. Jer. 34:18-19).

Now, compare the elements of the covenant as viewed in chapter 17.

The covenant promises are given in verses 1-8. Similar to chapter 15, these promises are of a great posterity, that Elohim shall be a God to Abram, and that he shall possess the land of Canaan. The covenant ritual of circumcision is set forth in verses 9-14, the heir is promised in verses 15-22, and obedience to God's command is recorded in verses 23-27. The Priestly account shows how quickly Abraham obeyed the commandment of God in respect to the covenant token. This probably implies that Abraham intended to do all in his power to walk blamelessly before God.

Skinner[51] has been most helpful in drawing the similarities

---

[51]Skinner, op. cit., pp. 276-298.

between chapters 15 and 17. In both accounts, Yahweh appears to Abram as the God of power. This emphasis on power is seen in the very name used in 17:1. Yahweh describes himself as *El Shaddai,* i.e., "God Almighty," or "God of All Might." A similar note is sounded by the use of the word "shield" (*magen*) in 15:1. Its root means "to cover, surround, defend, or protect." It is the kind of physical protection which an army could give.[52] And certainly this promise of power or defense was appropriate when one remembers that the fears of Abraham carried over from chapter 14.

As to the making of the covenant, although the ritual is different, in both cases similar elements are included. God gave the commands as to what was to be done (15:9; 17:10). Furthermore, God bound himself to the keeping of the covenant. In chapter 15:17, this was signified by "passing through" the animals. It is impossible to ascertain all that this implies, but in some way the action was a binder. Two possibilities are relevant, both of which should probably be united into one. Those who walked through the animals did so in order to invoke upon themselves similar fate to that of the slain animals, if they failed to observe their part of the agreement. Thus, God was, in effect, saying that if this promise does not hold, then I am not God! Another aspect is that the split animals probably represented the two parties of the covenant. Those "passing through" made all into a united whole; they became as one. This principle of the binding of the covenant occurs in 17:2 when the Lord says, "and I [myself] will make [give, set, put, establish] my covenant." It is also important to note that in both chapters there are the three specific promises of a son, a large posterity, and a land. In both, the "land" receives prominence as that place where fellowship shall exist between God and the covenant keepers. Although expressed differently, Abraham's initial inability to fathom so great a

---

[52]Brown, Driver, and Briggs, *op. cit.,* p. 171.

promise is expressed. In chapter 15:8 it is to be seen in his request for a sign, while in chapter 17:17 it is the expression of laughter.

Because of the similarities in form and emphasis in the chapters, the present writer's judgment is that here are two accounts of the same covenant, each presenting details which the other leaves out. They are two sides of the one coin. The ceremony of chapter 15 places emphasis upon the initiation of the pact, while chapter 17 stresses the possible perpetuation of that covenant through the rite of circumcision. In a sense, one stresses the blueprint of the covenant, while the other stresses its actuality. Chapter 15 announces that God gave the covenant in response to faith, while the picture is completed in chapter 17, which proclaims in its circumcision rite that God *demands* something in return.

Both sources are needed in order to give the completed emphasis. Consequently, the import of both chapters is that this is Abram's reward for making the right choice and taking the right steps. The Lord could not use Lot, but he could use Abraham in covenant history.

Covenant application.—An understanding of the place of the covenant in God's plan of redemption demands that some attention be given to the meaning and application of the covenant. The word "covenant" (*berith*) is actually used once in chapter 15 and eleven times in chapter 17.

Generally, the making of a covenant is referred to as "cutting a covenant" (cf. Gen. 26:28; Ex. 34:10). The expression "cutting a covenant" may have come from the practice of slaying, or cutting, victims in order to have blood with which to "seal" the covenant; or, it may refer to cutting the animals open, such as in Genesis 15, with those who make the agreement walking through as a symbol that they have become one.

It could also refer to the engraving of the covenant or contract on clay, stone, flesh, or upon whatever other material it could be engraved. The *berith*, that which is cut, probably comes from the root *barah*, which means basically "to bind or fetter together." Thus, a covenant is a binder.   A. B. Davidson thinks the notion of a bond "more nearly expresses the various uses of *berith* than any other word."[53] The term is used not only when two parties reciprocally bind themselves together but also when one party imposes a bond upon the other or when a party assumes a bond upon itself.   That the term was so understood by the Septuagint translators is seen in that of the 280 times the term occurs in the Old Testament, in all but 6 it is translated by the Greek *diathēkē* (from *dia* "two" and *tithēmi*, "put, place, arrange").   Thus, a covenant is something placed between two, a binding contract between two parties.

That the idea of covenant was used a long while before the time of Abraham is perhaps well known.   As early as the Mari tablets of the third millennium B.C., animals were being killed as a means of sealing a covenant.   The Syrian Qatna documents of the fifteenth century B.C. use the word *be-ri-ti*, certainly our word *berith*.   As recorded in his *Folk-Lore in the Old Testament*,[54] Frazer lists four covenant ceremonies, approximating that of Genesis 15, in Greece, Rome, Tibet, East Africa, South America, Assyria, Madagascar, Burma, Arabia, and elsewhere.   This is not an isolated phenomenon with which the Bible deals.

Almost universally, and certainly here, the covenant involved obligations, although it is possible that certain stipulations of the covenant are binding only upon one of the parties to the covenant.   This seems to be the case here.   Symbolically, only Yahweh passed between the animal parts (chapter 15), for he alone contracts obligations.   This is emphasized again in 17:7, which does not read "let us make a covenant," but rather, "I will make or give a covenant."   This was something

---

[53]A. B. Davidson, *The Theology of the Old Testament* (Edinburgh: T. & T. Clark, 1904), pp. 239 f.
[54]James George Frazer, *Folk-Lore in the Old Testament* (London: Macmillan & Co., Ltd., 1919), I, 391-428.

which by grace God was handing down to Abraham. God made it binding upon himself, but he did not make it binding upon the recipient. Abraham could not invalidate the covenant, although of course he could so neglect it as to fail to participate in its benefits.

However, it is quite clear that if the individual is to reap the benefits of the covenant, certain things are required. One requirement was to walk before God—"walk before me, and be blameless" (17:1, RSV). The Hebrew form of the verb used here is *hithpael*, thus implying habit. Make an effort to walk habitually before God, that is, to realize continually God's presence is the intent. The last part of the phrase "be blameless" carries with it the idea of wholeheartedness.

There must be an entire surrender of being. For Abraham to realize the benefits of the covenant meant for him to make God's will his law! This was to involve an active life with God. A further obligation was that Abram should participate in the covenant sign of circumcision (17:9-14). Apparently, drastic action was to be taken if one refused to participate in and submit to the rite. Excommunication from the community of the covenant people was the end result.

The larger implications of the covenant sign demand more detailed scrutiny. It is a mistake to believe that circumcision was a new rite introduced into Israel through Abraham. It was practiced by nearly all ancient people, the Philistines being the only notable exception. It is said that even today one-seventh of mankind uses the rite for one reason or another. Perhaps its most ancient use was in Egypt, for a relief at Saqqara in Egypt establishes the practice there as early as *ca.* 3400 B.C. In the biblical text, Jeremiah refers to the Egyptians as circumcised (Jer. 9:25-26).

Among these ancient people, the rite generally was used for one or all of three reasons. Often a utilitarian purpose was involved from the standpoint of personal cleanliness, hygiene, health, and sanitation. Some sacrificial element often entered into the rite, the idea being that a man sacrificed part of himself to God, thus shedding his own blood and establishing a blood covenant. In nearly all places, it was in some sense an initiatory rite, initiating one either into an adult life or into the mysteries of his religion.

But to say that the covenant and circumcision were known among others does not mean that the two had the same significance for Israel as for others. As was true of baptism in the New Testament, so in the Old Testament, an old symbol was taken but new and fuller meaning was poured into it.

The following elements seem to have been involved in the establishment of the covenant circumcision with Abraham.

(1) It was a continual reminder not only to God but, of more importance, to Abraham.

(2) It was an indication of the perpetual nature of the covenant. Even as human life was passed on from generation to generation, so this covenant was to be kept from generation to generation. In chapter 17, note the change of personal pronoun from the second person *singular* to the second person *plural* following verse 10. Abraham's seed were to "keep on keeping" the covenant. Note that in verse 10 the pronoun "you" is used for emphasis' sake. This perhaps was a hint to Abram that it would not be perpetuated among the descendants unless Abraham *kept* it.

(3) Circumcision was an indication of the living nature of the covenant. This covenant was not just a ritual to be performed; it symbolized a life to be lived "in" the covenant. Thus, the mark of the covenant was written in the living flesh and not on clay or stone tablets.

(4) Circumcision served as an act of purification and dedication. Many of the surrounding people used it as a puberty rite. However, for the Jews it was to be kept on the eighth day of the child's life as an act of dedication to Yahweh. To be sure, this in some sense meant the dedication of the child's parents to a reaffirmed covenant purpose, but it probably meant

more. In Hebrew psychology, performing a symbolic act to someone, or for someone, was thought to concretize and transfer the meaning of the act to its recipient. For a people corporately bound together, as the Hebrews were, this event in the child's life would perhaps be told him again and again. The very atmosphere of the retelling would lead the recipient to personal commitment.

(5) As an act of sacrifice in the giving of a portion of flesh, circumcision symbolized life.

(6) A shadow of the incarnation may also be seen in circumcision. Possibly this was what Marcus Dods[55] had in mind when he suggested that it was a sign of nature's unfitness to generate its own Saviour, thus showing the necessity of God's granting redemption. Regardless of Dod's intention, circumcision certainly points to the need for God to write his revelation in living flesh. This he later did in a noble way in the incarnation when the Son, the true revelation, took on human form. At least indirectly, therefore, the rudiments of this basic doctrine are to be found in the Old Testament rite of circumcision. In a sense, the covenant ceremony pointed to a redemptive need which could only be met as the divine united with the human.

Thus, one must see that circumcision was not simply ritual. From a theological standpoint, the Hebrew reflected upon it as an act of deep spiritual significance, having incorporated within it some of the basic principles of religion. The very essence of it all is summarized in Yahweh's divine "to be God to you" (17:7). It was a symbol of grace, fellowship, and communion with God.

Pertinent to the discussion of the covenant, in connection with God's answer to the need of man, is the question of for whom the covenant was intended. A special place was reserved for Abraham and Sarah. This was the significance

---

[55]Marcus Dods, "The Book of Genesis," *The Expositor's Bible* (London: Hodder & Stoughton, 1891), I, 167.

of the name change[56] (17:5,15). Etymologically, the names "Abram" and "Abraham" mean approximately the same. Simpson thinks that the change may reflect the Jewish custom of renaming a child at the time of circumcision, the time when he was brought into the covenant of which circumcision is the sign.[57] Abraham was a grown man, but there was a name change when he became a "child" of the covenant. Sarai's name was changed to "Sarah," meaning "princess" in the changed form. The etymology of "Sarai" is obscure, but, apparently, the change also gave her some special place in the covenant. Verse 16 would indicate such, although some have changed the pronoun of the Masoretic text from a blessing upon her (Sarah) to a blessing on him (the son). The blessing upon Abraham and Sarah is at the same time enlarged to include all men of faith (17:12-13). It does not hint at, nor involve, racial superiority or prejudice as was so well pointed out by Liston Pope in his book, *The Kingdom Beyond Caste*. It was a religious bond in which

no racial superiority is imputed, as the language of the covenant ("a multitude of nations") makes clear. Further, God went on to stipulate that every male entering the Hebrew community should be circumcised, "whether born in your house, or bought with your money from any foreigner who is not your offspring" (Genesis 17:12). The disavowal of a racial limitation could hardly be made more clear.[58]

This is to say that the covenant involved a universal theme for the redemptive inclusion of all. Literally, Abraham was to become the father of a "multitude of nations" (17:5,16). This is typified in the Arabians, who were his line through Keturah; the Ishmaelites, through Hagar; the Edomites, through his

---

[56]Up to this point the names "Abram" and "Abraham" have been variously used but henceforth the author will consistently use "Abraham."

[57]Simpson, *op. cit.*, pp. 609 f.

[58]Liston Pope, *The Kingdom Beyond Caste* (New York: Friendship Press, 1957), p. 148.

grandson, Esau; and, of course, the Jews through Sarah.

The result of Abraham's intimate connection with the covenant initiation was that he came to be called the "friend of God" by later writers.[59] Adolf Deissmann[60] suggests that the term probably meant that Abraham was God's favorite. Among the Ptolemies in Egypt at a much later period, it was a title of honor given to the highest royal officials. Persians and Greeks used it in the same fashion. Thus, Abraham as "God's friend" was one especially honored by God. Bowman's comment is appropriate at this point:

> In the earlier Old Testament literature Abraham is simply called God's "servant" (Gen. 26:24), which in the Hebrew idiom would have the same sort of semi official titular sense as that above indicated for "friend" in another cultural ethos. In both cases the thought would be that Abraham had a status of great importance in God's sight, that man's Sovereign had chosen him for service of real significance in His dominions.[61]

Thus, as a result of having made the right choice, Abraham was reassured that God would use him for a purpose. The same Lord who brought Abraham from his homeland (15:7) was to be with him yet. God's friend could depend on personal care, personal education, personal communion, and personal love. This was what calmed any fears and doubts which Abraham might have had, for as Voegelin says:

> In Genesis 15 the decisive step of liberation occurs, when Yahweh makes his berith with Abram. The worldly situation, to be sure, remains what it is for the time being; but spiritually the bondage is broken with the change of berith-masters. The order in which Abram lives from now on has been transformed from the Canaan of the Baal to the domain of Yahweh. The symbol of bondage has become the symbol of freedom. On this occasion, furthermore,

---

[59]Cf. 2 Chron. 20:7; Isa. 41:8; James 2:23.

[60]Adolf Deissmann, *Bible Studies* (Edinburgh: T. & T. Clark, 1901), pp. 167 f.

[61]Bowman, *op. cit.*, p. 178.

the peculiar nature of a berith with Yahweh reveals itself. In the mundane situation of Abram, as we said, nothing has changed. The new domain of Yahweh is not yet the political order of a people in Canaan; at the moment it does not extend beyond the soul of Abram. It is an order that originates in a man through the inrush of divine reality into his soul and from this point of origin expands into a social body in history.[62]

A summary word for the result of the covenant is "blessing," and this blessing was to come through an emphasis upon the *power* of God. This seems to be one of the prominent aspects of the blessing. In chapter 15, God tells Abraham that he is his "shield," in chapter 17 he tells him that he is "God Almighty"; and later in chapter 18, which also has to do with the initial reception of the covenant and of the heir through which it is to come, when some doubt was expressed by both Sarah and Abraham, then the Lord replied, "Is anything too hard for the Lord?" (18:14). The word used is *h*ᵉ*yipale*. It is the same root used in Isaiah 9 to describe the coming Messiah, the *wonderful* counselor. God tells Abraham at this point that he specializes in doing the extraordinary! The miraculous grace and power of God is emphasized throughout the Abrahamic narrative. That he could pick anyone out of such a polytheistic environment and use that one to initiate a process of redemption is miraculous.

Remembering then that this section shows the redemption whereby God began to meet the need as outlined in chapters 1-11, the emphasis is that *redemption is by the wonderful intervention of God.* The sinful condition of all mankind can be met because God has the power to do it.

Nothing has been said about the method whereby Abraham perceived the communion reported in chapters 15 and 17. The preface to chapter 15 flatly states that it was a vision. Verses 12 and 17 indicate that sleep had something to do with the process. No doubt Abraham had been doing much medi-

---

[62]Voegelin, *op. cit.*, p. 194.

tation and reflection upon the ways of God. Building upon this meditation, he came to a conscious realization through sleep. Probably he subsequently slew the animals as a symbolic representation to God that he understood and responded to his call.

The import of this basic beginning in Hebrew life can be indicated partially by reference to remarks which Albright wrote in 1957 as a new introduction to his book *From the Stone Age to Christianity:*

Turning to Israel, I defend the substantial historicity of patriarchal tradition, without any appreciable change in my point of view, and insist, just as in 1940-46, on the primacy of oral tradition over written literature. . . .

I now recognize that Israelite law and religious institutions tend to be older and more continuous than I had supposed . . . .

I recognized that the Covenant is not only fully as ancient as I had thought, but was much more pervasive in its effect on the religious and political life of Israel.[63]

Chapters 18-19

In a sense these two chapters continue the contrasted ends predicted upon the earlier choices of Lot and Abraham. Although the bulk of the story is geared to the trouble in Sodom and Gomorrah and Lot's fate, there penetrates the higher note of covenant promise to Abraham as a reward for his bold faith. The events which form the frame for the story do not come with much surprise, for the hint and groundwork had already been laid in chapter 13:12 f., which states that Lot "moved his tent as far as Sodom. Now the men of Sodom were wicked, great sinners against the Lord."

How long after chapter 14 these events transpired it is impossible to know, but, evidently, the best chronology would connect chapters 14, 15, 17 and chapters 18 and 19 in close

---

[63]William Foxwell Albright, *From the Stone Age to Christianity* (2d ed.; Garden City: Doubleday & Co., Inc., 1957), pp. 2 ff.

proximity. Of course, enough time has transpired now for Lot to obtain a status of stability within the community (19:1). One can suggest that these events happened some fifteen years after those of chapter 16, for there Abraham was eighty-five; here he is ninety-nine.

A brief review of the narrative with an indication of the change of speakers might prove of help. Three men (*'anoshim*) appeared to Abraham one day as he sat by his tent door. Abraham graciously entertained and fed them. *They* then asked for Sarah (18:9), and *he* (18:10) said that he would turn and bless Sarah. Then Yahweh (18:14) said, "Is anything too hard for the Lord?" Then Yahweh, after these *men* had gone on to Sodom (18:16 ff.), revealed to Abraham that Sodom and Gomorrah were to be destroyed (18:20). Although the *men* went on their way, there were *two angels* who arrived in Sodom in the evening. However, the people of the city recognized these as *men* (19:5) who were spending the night with Lot. They told Lot that they were going to destroy the wicked place because its evil had gone up to Yahweh. Lot was told by them to escape to a mountain, but he begged to be allowed to go to a certain nearby city. In making this particular request, Lot addressed *them* as O Lord (singular). Reporting the reply, the text has, "*He* said to him, 'Behold *I* grant you this favor also.'" (19:21). *Yahweh* then brought fire and brimstone upon the cities and destroyed them (19:24 ff.).

The vacillation between the identification of the characters as first several, then one, calls for some clarification. Numerous attempts have been made in an effort to identify the "three men." Perhaps the most common view is that these were *Yahweh* and *two angels*. However, it is to be objected that God should be presented as so casually walking with men, and it is a stretch even of the device of anthropomorphism to picture God as eating. At no other place in the Old Testament does such a shocking figure occur. Furthermore, such an identification would reveal a God who is not "all seeing," for he had to go down to Sodom in person to ascertain what was taking place. Yet, the God who sees all (*El Roi*) is integral to Old Testament thought.

According to the pointing of the Masoretic text, Abraham addressed the men as "Lord," thus implying that Abraham recognized Yahweh as one of the three. However, it could easily be that this should be "Lords" or "Sirs," plural, thus restoring, with the Samaritan Pentateuch, the plural throughout. Of course, the text as presented by the Masoretes does at times have the plural (19:2). Finally, the changeable way by which description is given would rule out the suggestion of angels. In 18:2,16,22; 19:5,8,10,12 they are called *men*, while only in two verses are they called *angels* (19:1,15). Although it is true that the motif of entertaining strangers, unaware that they are divine, is a common one to ancient literature,[64] the popular solution of calling this setting *mythological* and casting it aside will not suffice either. This is the attempted solution sometimes called the "expansion theory." The basic idea is that there was a folk tale which originally had as its purpose the telling of a story about a hero (Abraham) who was so great that he could get what he wanted from God himself. Supposedly, during the prophetic period, the narrative was edited in such a way that it was made also to teach a fine lesson about God. This literary adaptation would account for the differences in pronouns and persons observed in the story.

A popular tradition among early Christians with reference to the passage might be called that of "Trinitarian implication." This was popular among such apologists as Justin Martyr in his *Dialogue Against Trypho* and in Ignatius' *Epistle to the Magnesians*. In this particular section of Genesis, they see the second person of the Trinity—God—abiding in flesh and walking on the earth. However, it is hardly necessary to sug-

---

[64]Hermann Gunkel, *The Legends of Genesis*, trans. W. H. Carruth (Chicago: Open Court, 1901), pp. 93-95.

gest that since the doctrine of the Trinity was not formulated until the days of the early church, to attribute a New Testament formulation to an Old Testament setting is eisegesis.

It would be fair to say that as one considers this passage in connection with the larger biblical context, reading backwards, one can see something of a preview of the incarnation implied; that is, the need of God to come in the flesh and deal with his creatures, but this was not the primary usage to which the compiler put chapters 18 and 19.

There remains, then, the suggestion which the present author would make as an attempted solution, and it might be called the "extension of Yahweh" concept. God in the Old Testament is represented as extending himself into this world in many ways. His name, for example, represents his personality (Psalm 20:1; Ex. 12:1,11; 14:24-25). The ark embodies his presence (1 Sam. 4:5-8).

Now these characters in this immediate story are sometimes called men and sometimes called angels. However, the word translated "angels" also may be just as well translated "messenger." Here then, there are three messengers, or representatives, through whom God is working. God so controlled these men that he could be represented as dwelling in them, speaking through them, and they could be pictured as speaking *for* Yahweh. This really is not strange, for a similar usage is prominent in the New Testament. Paul in Galatians 2:20 could say: "I have been crucified with Christ; and it is no longer I that live, but Christ liveth in me: and that life which I now live in the flesh I live in faith, the faith which is in the Son of God who loved me, and gave himself up for me." Although not in the same sense of fulness involved in the New Testament concept, God so related himself to his messengers[65] that they could speak directly for God. With such an understanding, the vacillation in terms is not perplexing.

---

[65]It must not be forgotten that *melakim,* translated "angels," literally means "messengers."

More specifically, in chapter 19, the theme of Lot's degeneration, as emphasized in chapter 13, is renewed. To associate
and walk with ungodly men is to absorb their influence and
eventually to stand in the way in which they stand and ultimately to sit in the very seat of the scornful ones. Lot had
reached the second step, and God in his grace was going to
rescue him before he went the remainder of the way.

An indication of the kind of people with whom Lot lived is
to be seen in this chapter. The word translated "know" in verses
5 and 8 is habitually used in the Old Testament in the sense
of "knowing a person carnally," (Gen. 4:1,17,25; 24:16; 38:26;
1 Sam. 1:19; Judg. 19:25; 1 Kings 1:4; Num. 31:17-18,35).

In this immediate context, base men of the city are so
disrespectful of the guests as to desire to treat them in an
unnatural and lustful fashion. This may be a subtle way of
suggesting that since these visitors represented the divine,
the population was so base that it had absolutely no respect
for that which represented the divine will and way. It is also
another passage lending description and credence to the
author's major theme—the need for redemption.

Lot's willingness to sacrifice his daughters made it neither
right nor desirable, but in accord with that society, it was
considered the lesser of two evils. Lot desired to be a coura-
geous champion of the obligations of hospitality in a situation
of extreme embarrassment. Since women in those days were
regarded primarily as chattel or property, Lot cannot be
blamed too much for his willingness to sacrifice his daughters.
That he would capitulate so readily, however, does indicate his
lack of genuine stamina and courage. Perhaps this desire to
sacrifice everything needful in order to have all to "go right"
was his downfall. He really wanted the approval of these two
messengers of Yahweh. This desire for approval may have
been the reason he made such a choice in the first place.

The theme of the remaining portion of the chapter is that of
judgment upon wickedness. That something drastic hap-

pened, there can be no doubt. There was an unusual catastrophe of such great nature that it remained forever fixed in men's minds; for according to 19:24: "Then Jehovah rained upon Sodom and upon Gomorrah brimstone and fire from Jehovah out of heaven; and he overthrew those cities." The Hebrew root of "rained" is sometimes used as something sent by an extraordinary and supernatural power. Here the *hiphil* or "caustive" Hebrew form is used, which is a way of saying that whatever happened, it happened because God was behind it. This was the work of God in judging and punishing sin.

The theological theme and purpose of judgment has been established. This is in no way injured when one asks, from a physical standpoint, whether there is any explanation possible for the physical phenomenon which became the vehicle of the religious theme. Some have suggested the possibility of volcanic activity, but geological surveys seem to rule this out. Apparently, there has been no volcanic activity in this area since *ca.* 4000 B.C. A better suggestion is that which was given by Strabo—that there probably was a great earthquake accompanied by lightning which brought utter ruin and a terrible conflagration to Sodom and the other communities in the vicinity. The destructive fire may have been caused by an ignition of gases and seepages of asphalt emanating from the region through lightning or more natural means. Credence to this suggestion is given by a report from F. G. Clapp, American geologist, who in 1936, after a study of the petroleum in the area, made this report:

Exudations of bitumen, petroleum and probably natural gas (since the last named is generally an accompaniment of these substances), emerging throughout historical times, may have been erratic and have taken place whenever disastrous earthquakes or controlling subterranean pressure impulses were manifested. The seepage, catching fire from lightning or human action, would adequately account for recorded phenomena without necessarily having recourse to supernatural or fanciful theories. . . . In this spot one still finds seepages of semi-fluid petroleum in the form of soft bitumen saturating tarry conglomerates of late Tertiary or Recent age, which have a reported volume . . . of nearly 750,000 cu. ft. containing 140,000 cu. ft. of asphalt, emanating either from below the surface or from contiguous Senonian limestones.[66]

Remembering that this is the J source, it would not be so surprising that the writer used the anthropomorphic "rained" to describe what took place. But in no sense does this rule out the miraculous or God's guidance, for the miracle was in the "timing" at which the so-called "natural" event transpired.

The theological premise of judgment upon sin is continued by another element in the story which, though theologically factual, may not be historically factual. This has to do with Lot's wife becoming a pillar of salt (19:26). This is probably an interpolation or at least an accretion to the original story. When the nearby "salt mountain," Jebul Usdum (Arabic: mountain of Sodom) was noticed, there developed the tradition that this was what happened to Lot's wife; and thus, although perhaps not exactly historical, it becomes an important part of the story and emphasizes the disastrous results which befall any who refuse to make a clean break with sin.

Something of the growing nature of sin is to be faced again in the account of Lot's sinful relationship with his daughters (19:30-38). Verses 37 and 38 denote this as an account of the origin of the Moabites and the Ammonites, apparently an accurate account. At the same time, it must be remembered that the Hebrews were always at strife with these groups. Maybe it was one way of saying that seed sown in such sinful beginnings always leads to disastrous results.

When in 19:31 the daughters are reported to have said,

---

[66]Frederick G. Clapp, "Geology and Bitumens of the Dead Sea Area, Palestine and Transjordan," *The Bulletin of the American Association of Petroleum Geologists,* XX (1936), 881-909 Quoted by J. Pemose Harland in "The Destruction of the Cities of the Plain," *The Biblical Archaeologist,* VI (September, 1943), 49.

"there is not a man in the earth," it may have been simply a way of saying, "we are the survivors of a universal catastrophe." The tragedy was so great that initially this was the belief. The character of Lot was bolstered somewhat in the incident, for, apparently, he regarded the suggestion of his daughters with great disfavor; for they had to intoxicate Lot before they could use him for their purpose (19:32).

In the larger narrative, Abraham's basis of intercession is, "Shall not the Judge of all the earth do right?" (18:25). He proceeded to pray from his knowledge that God is a righteous God and that God's concept of justice was far superior to his own.

Abraham's answer did not come in the way that he had expected. Abraham looked (19:28) and the smoke of the land went up. No doubt he immediately thought that Lot was lost and that his prayer had not been answered. But God had answered already by the delivery of Lot. One must not overlook the spirit which made such effective prayer possible. Certainly Abraham held nothing of the episodes of the past against Lot, else he never would have been able to pray this way. The concept that grace is mingled with judgment also penetrates the story. Where there is a wicked Sodom, God sends his servants to warn; that is, he gives man a fair chance to prepare (cf. Amos 3:6 ff.). The decision as to what man shall do is up to man, even as it was with Lot in this case. Tragically, the reaction to God's grace is that man often sins again, as was true with Lot and his daughters. This cycle occurs again and again.

Finally, from a larger perspective, the setting of chapters 18 and 19 provides another opportunity of saying that God would redeem all of sinful humanity possible, and that a covenant people must agonize with him as a means of bringing such redemption to fruition. Man must, however, individually decide whether he will be or will not be a participant in this redemption.

The Weakness of Man and Trouble (16; 21)

Although chapters 16 and 21 cannot have been exactly the same event from the standpoint of time, for in the earlier chapter Hagar is pregnant, while in the later she has already delivered her son, yet they do form a single picture in the common theme of God's compassionate concern for the oppressed of the earth and of trouble as an accompaniment of man's sin. What is presented here is a sustained picture of a grievous wound which can be directly traced to Abraham's earlier lapse of faith on his sojourn into Egypt. It will not be difficult to see that similar emphases pervade both settings. The significance of the name Ishmael, "God hears," is given major attention (16:11; 21:17). This is to suggest to all needy men that God sees, hears, and aids in times of affliction and trouble. There is a sound of universality about this; here is one who is not pure Hebrew but Egyptian—one who is not among the "Chosen," yet, she is blessed with the presence of the covenant God. There is a note of compassionate concern, for here is one who has been mistreated by man, yet she is cared for and well treated by God.

In both passages, there is drawn a description of the mode of life and the characteristics of Abraham's descendants (16:12; 21:20). There is a contrast of the kind of life these two boys were destined to live. One would become skilled in outdoor life because he was forced to follow that kind of existence. Isaac would live in the sheltered protection of a favorite son at home. The suggestion here is that environment has had much to do with the way the two groups of people, descendants of Ishmael and Isaac, have turned out. The Ishmaelites were always a more or less nomadic group.

Also given a marked note of emphasis is the sacredness of a certain well which was consecrated by a theophany (16:7,14; 21:19). There is no way to get away from it. The Old Testament emphasizes places where encounters with God have taken place as special places and memorable shrines. The purpose in this was that when a nation was oppressed and about to forget all that God had done through the years, there was nothing like going back in memory to an earlier place of encounter between God and man. The existentialist development of a God of "encounter" can trace its roots to the Old Testament.

Problems of Chronology and Translation

The age of Ishmael has been a source of perennial difficulty both to translator and interpreter. According to the Priestly chronology of chapter 16, Abraham was eighty-six years old when Ishmael was born (16:16; 17:25). In turn, Abraham was one hundred years old when Isaac was born. The weaning festival which is implied in chapter 21, usually took place when the child was about three years old. Thus, Ishmael must have been seventeen when he and his mother were cast out into the wilderness. At first glance, and because of the way it has been translated, the Elohistic chronology of chapter 21 seems to give a different picture. There the picture is presented of the *child* placed under the bushes and its mother cried, "Let me not look upon the death of the *child*" (21:16). It is said that God heard the voice of the *lad* (21:17). But contrary to appearance, there is no discrepancy here. The word used in Genesis 21:15-16 is the Hebrew *yeled*, which basically means child, son, boy, youth, or descendants in general. At times it is used even of people of some age. It was so used of the person whom Lamech slew (4:23) and of the ones from whom Rehoboam took counsel (1 Kings 12:8) and of a poor wise youth in Ecclesiastes 4:12. In verse 18, the word used is *na'ar, which means boy, lad, or youth. Na'ar can be used of one of marriageable age (Gen. 34:19). The warrior Absalom could be so designated (2 Sam. 18:5,12). The term was also used of Zadok, a young man of valor (1 Chron. 12:28). From the possible translations, it is impossible to conclude other than that the translators were careless in their choice of words and that when the terms *yeled* and *na'ar* are rightly understood, there is less conflict between the chronologies of chapters 16 and 21.

A further question of text is the question of "who wept" in chapter 21:16. The translations, following the Greek rendering, usually read, "the *child* lifted up his voice and wept." However, the Hebrew text reads, ". . . she [Hagar] lifted up her voice and wept." Now the reason the Greek is usually taken above the Hebrew is because of the statements in verses 15 and 18. Those two troublesome statements are these: "she *cast* the child under one of the bushes," and "Arise, lift up the lad, and hold him fast with your hand."

As for the word translated "cast" (*shalak*), the first thing to notice is that the word seems to come from a Phoenician or Aramaic background of dubious meaning. Most often it is translated as "throwing away, casting off, shedding, to throw away something." Now this would be a fairly ruthless way to put a child under a tree. It is to be doubted that such treatment would have been given this boy by his mother. There is a cognate root which is the same in sound (*shalach*), which is nearly always translated "send" or "send away." Probably that is the word intended and the meaning intended here. Hagar "sent" Ishmael to sit in the shade of a tree, while she did some serious thinking.

The word for "lift up" in verse 18 is *nasa,'* which means "to take up, lift up, bear, carry, graciously receive, or hold in honor."[67] Thus, verse 18 may simply be saying, "Hold on to the boy, watch after him, honor him, and something honorable will come from the situation." The next phrase in the verse seems to reinforce this interpretation. *Chazak*, translated here as "hold fast," has the root meaning of "strengthen, grow firm, prevail, hold firmly to"; and in at least one place it means "to devote one's self to." Thus, the last half of the verse, in

---

[67] Brown, Driver, and Briggs, *op. cit.*, p. 670.

keeping with good Hebrew parallelism, reinforces the first half.

One further comment of this nature is necessary. The ninth verse of chapter 21 suggests that Sarah saw Ishmael "playing" with Isaac. The word used here is *m^etsacheq*. In the Hebrew structure of the word known as "piel," and used here, it means to "jest" or "play," even in the sense of scoffing. Thus, it is possible to understand, since P's chronology makes Ishmael about seventeen years of age at the time, the traditional Jewish interpretation of Ishmael "as a rude lad scoffing at the family joy." Paul, in Galatians 4:29, so alludes to Ishmael as persecuting Isaac. Chances are, then, that verse 9 should read "scoffing" or "mocking" rather than "playing." The reader will notice also from the Revised Standard Version footnote that "with her son Isaac" is lacking in the Hebrew text.

From the vantage point outlined, it will be understood that both chapters 16 and 21 are included in the records as a means of stressing this tension within Abraham's house as having been habitual over a period of many years.

Principles and Practices

As was suggested earlier, the background to the incidents in chapters 16 and 21 is to be traced to Abraham's early sojourn into Egypt (Gen. 12). He is now reaping the fruit of his wandering experience. Far more, this original Egyptian defection became the basis of a second defection. Even the vessels whom God binds to himself in a covenant experience are imperfect. The two chapters lend emphasis to the maxim that "what one sows, one reaps."

It is very evident in chapter 16 that Abraham tried the way of expediency rather than the way of faith. The promised son had been delayed, and each passing day increased the ugliness of the terrible stigma attached to barrenness by the Hebrews. Abraham regretted this and Sarai probably was afraid that unless she did something, Abraham might actually leave her for another. As a result of such thought, plans were made for Abraham to produce an heir through Hagar. This practice in itself was not an unusual one. Indeed, it was an accepted custom of the day. Thus, one passage in the Nuzi material reads: "If Kelim-ninu [the bride] does not bear [children], Kelim-ninu shall acquire a woman of the land of Lullu [where the choicest slaves were obtained] as a wife for Shennima [the bridegroom]."[68] These instructions are similar to those given by Sarai to Abraham (16:2). The child born through such a practice was generally "adopted" by the barren wife and considered her own child. There are numerous allusions in literature of an early, primitive ceremony of adoption, in which the child of the handmaiden was actually brought forth on the knees of a barren woman as a sign of adoption. In other words, the knees of a barren woman would serve as the delivery table for a new child. Thereby, the new child was duly and legally adopted (cf. Gen. 30:3). It means here that Ishmael should have been acknowledged as Sarai's own child, but, of course, it is evident from what follows (16:4) Sarai developed a different spirit and reneged on the ceremony.

Suffering immediately followed Abraham's hearkening to Sarai's voice rather than God's. There was the natural jealousy which caused turmoil in the household. As is usually characteristic when sin captures people, there was a shifting of responsibility so that Sarai blamed Abraham and Abraham blamed Sarai. The end result was that Abraham tried to "buy peace at any price" (16:6), and thereby evade his responsibility.

There is much in the story that is so characteristically human. Finding herself pregnant, Hagar perhaps became quite insolent toward her mistress, no doubt flaunting her superiority because of her ability to conceive. The feeling of enmity must have increased when years later Sarah realized that she,

---

[68]Pritchard, *op. cit.*, p. 220.

too, could give birth to a child! Isaac was born; and as increased favoritism and protection were given to Isaac, more tension developed. Time for the family weaning festival came, perhaps then as now in Palestine, when Isaac was three years old (cf. 1 Sam. 1:22). When Sarah saw the young man Ishmael scoffing at her beloved (21:9), it proved too much, and the final breach between Sarah and Hagar was consummated. Imagine Abraham's predicament—his involvement, his trial, and his pain—as he tried to handle the situation. In desperation, he and Sarah sent Hagar and Ishmael away (21:10 ff.). This, too, was a violation of the ethical standard of the day, for contracts between handmaidens and their mistresses specified that the handmaid's offspring should not be sent away. Maybe, this was why Abraham refused to comply with Sarah's request until he at least felt that he had some word from the Lord about his entire ordeal.

No effort is made in the Scriptures to vindicate Hagar, but she was, in some sense, a victim of circumstances. Even outcasts and foreigners, such as was Hagar, came under the surveillance and compassion of the covenant God. Although Hagar was a "nobody," God heard her cry (12:17), spoke to her (21:17), provided for her (21:19), assured her (21: 17 f.), and granted her the understanding of his comforting presence. "God opened her eyes" (21:19); she saw God (16:13). Through the actions of God, her eyes were turned from self-pity to see God. Is this what God, through the covenant, desired to do for all?

The Supreme Test of Faith (22)

One would think that Abraham had faced enough to purify him from all dross and prepare him and his people for covenant commitment and transference, but the worst was yet to come. However, it is not difficult to find the basic purpose of this particular trial. In the Scripture writer's use of the story, at least, it was a great testing, trial, proving in Abraham's life.

It was indeed a proving! Abraham was to be used for a great purpose. Did he have the stuff which made him usable? It must not be forgotten, as is indicated by the first verse, that in some way it was God who was doing the proving. The word used is *nisah,* a *piel* form of the Hebrew verb which means "really tried, proved, tested." The same word is used in Exodus 17:7, where the children of Israel put the Lord "to the proof." The children of the Lord put God to the test; they were proving to see whether he really could and would provide as he said. God now is putting Abraham to the test, proving him, to see whether he really will stand true, even as he had promised to do—will he do it when doing it is hard and difficult and costly? Has he actually surrendered his will to the will of God? Is his character well established; has he surrendered all? Or, is he at least willing to surrender all? Thus, the incident is called by some the highest personal moment of faith in the Old Testament.

The Reception of the Test

To analyze the substance of the test is easier than a solution as to how the test came. From a negative standpoint, it certainly was not a literal command to sacrifice a life. If it is so accepted, then Abraham, in obedience to the command of God, is represented as intending to commit the horrible crime of taking a human life, thus violating a principle earlier enunciated in Genesis 9:5-6. Such child sacrifice is always a cause for the denunciation of participant kings in the Book of the Kings (cf. 2 Kings 16:3). God does not test a man of faith with a command to do something that is morally wrong and contrary to the character of God. In fact, one of the strongest statements in the Old Testament for ascertaining whether something is the will or word or command of God is to ask whether it is in keeping with the character of God (Deut. 13:1 ff.). Furthermore, Mowinckel is correct in suggesting that testings which a man experiences in his life come in the form of an inner voice or stirring of soul rather than as a direct voice or command from heaven.[69]

Just from a human standpoint, it would be difficult to convince any godly person and loving parent that it was the will of God for him to sacrifice his child in a kind of deadly sacrifice which could be of no avail in service to God or to mankind.

Though there is nothing in the passage to suggest it, some commentators would infer, perhaps out of a desire to avoid the moral dilemma of a command from God for an immoral act, that this was actually a voice from Satan which God captivated and turned to his own glory, thus making the best out of a bad situation. Such demonic impressions were not unknown in the Old Testament revelation as evidenced by David's temptation to make a census (1 Chron. 21:1 f.). This suggestion is hardly acceptable, however, for there did not appear a developed doctrine of Satan in the Old Testament until about 400 B.C., just a little prior to the writing of the book of Chronicles. The material before us is from the E stratum, whose written form is to be dated in the vicinity of 750 B.C.

It must be remembered that the age in which Abraham lived was one in which his pagan neighbors often sacrificed their choicest children to their nonexistent gods as evidence of personal surrender, adoration, and commitment. Abraham, having viewed these who had less opportunity for comprehending God than he himself had, often must have asked himself whether he could give his only son. Had he surrendered his own will to such a degree of sacrifice? Perhaps he had asked himself, "Would I be willing, like my neighbors, to destroy with my own hands this one who represents my great hopes—actually the hope of the race?" Suddenly, what had been a thought of meditation gripped the inner being of Abraham until he thought he heard it as a clear call from God, "Go sacrifice Isaac." This was the fallible human reception of

---

[69]Sigmund Mowinckel, *The Old Testament as Word of God,* trans. Reidar B. Bjornard (New York: Abingdon Press, 1959), p. 96.

an infallible divine question which, in essence, asked, "Do you love me more than *him*, in spite of *him?*" Abraham understood it to mean that he physically had to give Isaac, when what God really was asking was in the realm of inner attitude.

The Nature of the Inner Test

Apparently, the "after these things" of 22:1 refers to the previous chapter (21:32-33), after Abraham had homesteaded himself a place at Beer-sheba. It looked as though he had things in good shape for living. Perhaps he thought he had arrived. Then, there was a severe test with no warning. There was in his life a principle often faced in ours. Life seems to never reach its climax; it is moving ever toward something else.

Note the graphic description of verse 2, "Take your son, your only son Isaac, whom you love" (RSV). This emphasizes the greatness of the sacrifice. Abraham felt that God was asking for the dearest that he had. Is not this so often the way it is? As Sören Kierkegaard has emphasized, "True surrender is indicated when man is willing to give God his 'Isaac.' "[70]

Enunciated early in man's part in the plan of redemption is this principle of the necessity of trusting obedience to the will of God with the surrender of every reservation. There is no service in the covenant commitment nor is there genuine joy in the covenant commitment until "the moment when we let go of ourselves and cast ourselves upon him and say an unreserved 'yes' to God and declare ourselves willing to do, by his help, all he may demand of us even though it be in fear and trembling."[71] This is the nature of the inner test which covenant commitment fosters. Like the book of Job at a later date, this story indicates that a trial can be a means of underscoring true devotion and piety.

---

[70]Cf. the keen understanding of what is involved in Sören Kierkegaard, *Fear and Trembling*, trans. Robert Payne (London: Oxford University Press, 1939).

[71]Mowinckel, *op. cit.*, p. 97.

Worthy Principles in the Test

It is not difficult to understand from the story that the best
one has belongs to God. Also included here is the first instance
of the principle of substitution in sacrifice. Here is a principle which one meets in various ways, shades, and varieties
throughout the remainder of the Bible. Indeed the complete
fulfilment of the covenant itself ultimately was dependent
upon a substitution in man's behalf. One will want to notice
also the number of times in the chapter that the phrase "The
Lord will provide" occurs. Have the right attitude and God
will provide. Sacrifice is effective because it is God who actually provides the grace, and, in this case, the actual sacrifice
which makes it effective. God accepts the inner attitude and
disposes himself to accept and provide the basic elements of
sacrifice. Thus, early the truth was taught that the essence of
sacrifice is the moral disposition of the giver (cf. Psalm
51:18-19).

The Locale of the Experience

There is this much of literal element in the incident—because he understood a sacrifice to be demanded, Abraham
made a journey somewhere. It is impossible, actually, to lo-
cate the place to which Abraham journeyed, and, really, it does
not matter. The emphasis is that he was willing to go! The
book of Chronicles puts the scene on the Temple mount at
Jerusalem. If this be the place, then the journey was indeed
a strange one and adds even more mystery to the incident.
Beer-sheba, where Abraham dwelled at the time, is in the
southern half of the country, some 40 miles from Jerusalem.
This was a long distance from home for a sacrifice. If the
interpretation of Genesis 14 is correct in the earlier part of the
book, then it is strange indeed that Abraham would go to a
territory where he had had a great difficulty with a local
religious situation to make a sacrifice which could mean nothing
to anyone but himself.

The Response of Abraham

Abraham *worshiped* (22:5). Certainly there was much about it that Abraham did not understand, but he wanted to go and worship.[72] This is but an indication of his willingness to submit to God's commands with complete obedience, worship, and trust. Abraham was *obedient*. Apparently, there was no arguing. Thinking that this was what God wanted, he rose early in the morning and did what he had to do. The emphasis upon morning may be an indication that the thought of the necessity of sacrificing Isaac occurred to Abraham during the night, possibly in a dream. As a consequence of it all, he was *blessed* (22:17). This verse says so little and yet it says so much. You can almost see the quickening of Abraham's step as he goes back home. Not only was he relieved at the way things had turned out but he was sure that he had learned something about the basic nature of a man's relationship, attitude, and disposition toward God.

Relation to Sacrifice in General

Just what Abraham had in mind when he went to sacrifice Isaac it is impossible to know. However, studies of sacrifice have revealed three basic attitudes; perhaps these were in the heart of Abraham. Often sacrifice seems to have been considered a *communion offering* that sought to bind the worshiper and the God together by the sharing in the body of the sacrificed. Again, sacrifice was a *gift* presented to God to induce him to act on behalf of the offerer, and again it seems to have been thought that sacrifice actually *released* vital power which could be infused into the life of the one who made the sacrifice. Whatever sacrifice generally meant, it seems to have been heightened and intensified in the attitude of Abraham.

In Semitic thought, there seems to have been special sig-

---

[72]The word is *shachah*, which basically means "to honor God with prayers, bow one's self down, prostrate one's self, do homage, submit one's self to."

nificance in the offering of the first child, or involving the same principle, in the giving of the first fruits. This was certainly true with reference to animals as can be found in Exodus 22: 28-29, but it seemed to apply to the offering of children also. In keeping with ancient belief, the Canaanites practiced the custom of giving the firstborn to their god. Excavations at Gezer and elsewhere reveal a cemetery of infants deposited in large jars underneath the floors of the temple—jars containing the remains of newborn infants. Fortunately, the Old Testament provides some relief from the custom, for instead of the firstborn child, there was to be substituted relief in the form of either animal substitute (Ex. 12:12-13; 34:20), a fixed payment to be made in place of the infant child (Num. 18:16), or perhaps Levites could take their place (Num. 3:11-13, 40-45). Who knows but that this experience in the life of Abraham provided the first insight which finally matured into a complete disavowal of child sacrifice among those who rightly understood the revelation of God?

Happiness in Life and in Death (23; 24:1-9; 25:1-11)

This material is intended to deal primarily with Abraham's closing days. However, a proper appreciation of his last years demands that some attention be paid to the patriarch's relationship to his friends throughout his life, for, in a measure, his happy life relationships prepared him for the satisfaction experienced in late and declining years. Since a time of old age is often a time of reminiscing, perhaps this is as good a place as any to pay tribute to some of those who had an especially close place to Abraham and then to look at the old patriarch's departure from these friends "to be gathered to his fathers."

His Companions

Eliezer, the good servant, certainly deserves recognition, although he is specifically mentioned only in chapters 15 and 24. He had been with Abraham for quite a while; he probably was chosen as Abraham passed through Damascus on his trip from Haran to Palestine. Throughout the narrative, he shows several excellent characteristics. Although not initially chosen as a member of the covenant family, he had contributed a long life of *faithful service to his master*. He was a steward when Isaac was born and was serving in the same capacity when Isaac was married. Always he seemed willing to remain in the background while contributing to the welfare and happiness of others. Had Isaac not been born, perhaps Eliezer would have received, if not all, a good share of the inheritance, but there seems to have been no resentment on his part. Dedicated to his mission (24:33), he humbled himself immediately in order to exalt his master. His service was done in such a way that all knew him as a man of trust.

The reader will notice that Abraham was quite concerned that Isaac not marry one of a Canaanite background (24:3). It was a serious matter to choose a wife for an only son, but more serious was the matter of obtaining a wife for Isaac, for she would be the mother of those who should carry on the covenant. This will indicate something of the confidence which Abraham placed in Eliezer. Eliezer's mission was sealed by a pledge which required the placing of his hand under the thigh of Abraham (24:9). Such pledges required the placing of the hand near the genitals, the life giving source; this is a pledge to be kept alive, fulfilled. Involved was a two-way encounter in which Eliezer assumed the burden of responsibility and Abraham said that he was willing to rest his full weight on Eliezer. Abraham's trust of Eliezer is further evidenced in the bestowal upon him of a wealth of materials and goods (24:10). Abraham certainly had no way of knowing whether Eliezer would come back, but he trusted him to transport the goods to Haran. Perhaps Abraham could trust Eliezer because the servant had proved to be a man of *religious faith*. The content of 24:12 would indicate that he had learned his faith from Abraham, his master.

Join the thought of this verse to that of verses 14 and 27 and there is emphasis upon Eliezer's confidence in the Lord's leadership and providence. As someone has suggested, he saturated his work with prayer and then waited upon God for direction—always a step of faith.

With just a few brief glimpses along the way, the reader is likely to have gained a very unfavorable impression of Sarah, for her anger and impatience in the Hagar-Ishmael episodes and her cynicism at the birth announcement of Isaac certainly are not symptoms of beautiful character. She must have caused Abraham many a heartache.

Nevertheless, there were other traits about Sarah which endeared her to her husband and served as a source of continual comfort to him until late years. Her ability to inspire the devotion of her husband is to be recognized in Abraham's genuine sorrow at her death. He had other wives, but not any who were as dear to him as Sarah (23:2). The patriarch's concern was punctuated by the tears which he shed (23:2). The words used with reference to his grief are interesting. The first, *lispodh,* indicates wailing, lamenting, smiting one's breast in great grief, while the second, *livkothah,* similarly indicates intense or bitter weeping.[73]

Something of Abraham's concern for Sarah is perhaps also to be noted in his diligent efforts to secure for her a burial place (23:3 ff.). He exerted his best tradesman or "merchant prince" abilities in the battle of wits with the Hittites. Now the Hittites were active as early as the eighteenth century B.C. in the Mesopotamian Valley area, although their native home was Asia Minor. Many believe that the Hittites settled in Palestine sometime in the Middle Bronze Age (2000-1500) probably in connection with the Hyksos.[74] The Tell El Amarna Letters reveal their presence there in 1375-1358 B.C.

---

[73]Cf. the use of the word in 1 Sam. 1:10; Jer. 22:10; and Lam. 1:2.

[74]Jack Finegan, *Light from the Ancient Past* (Princeton: Princeton University Press, 1946), p. 145.

Abraham's deal with Ephron, the Hittite, is usually viewed as an action on Ephron's part in order to get an excessive price. However, from Hittite material which has been found, it has been learned that the transfer of land among the Hittites carried with it certain feudal duties; i.e., there were certain services which the purchaser was obligated to perform for the people who lived on the land. If the buyer purchased a holding, he was obligated to fulfil these duties unless he bought only a portion of the land. It is very obvious here that Abraham was trying to do just that, that is, to buy only a portion of the land. But he was not successful. Apparently, Ephron wished to rid himself of any obligations to the people who lived on the land (23:11). Thus, as G. E. Wright says, "Abram became feudatory for the entire field."[75] There were services to the Hittites living there which he was binding himself by contract to perform. You can understand why Abraham, desirous of keeping a separation from the people of the land, trying to maintain purity to the covenant relation, would object to such an arrangement. However, possibly the authenticity of the arrangement is indicated in verse 17, where the trees on the land are mentioned. Hittite business documents, interestingly enough, list the exact number of trees in each real estate transaction. Abraham pressed himself to the extreme to care in the hour of death for the woman he loved.

Among the contributing factors giving cause to Abraham's concern was Sarah's beauty and culture. She, no doubt, had maintained something of the old culture from the land of Ur, and she was pretty in stature (Gen. 12:11,14). Far more, she was often willing to follow the leadership of her husband. Although one cannot place approval upon the deceit involved, in both chapters 12 and 20, Sarah is presented as obedient to the wishes of Abraham. Apparently, she followed Abraham wherever he went because she loved him. For his sake she

---

[75]Wright, *Biblical Archaeology*, p. 51.

left a cultured existence and became a pioneer. Intensifying Abraham's concern for Sarah was his appreciation of her very strong maternal fidelity (16 and 21), although at times it was expressed in poor fashion.

Shortly before his death, Abraham took another wife, Keturah (25:1). He had known the joy and comfort of married life in his home shared so long with Sarah and in his loneliness desired such warmth again. Not much is known about Keturah, although a tribe of Keturah has been found near the region of Mecca; so apparently tradition would point to her place of origin as north Arabia.

A son from this union was Shuah, who became important enough that he founded a people; for in the book of Job, one of the friends was Bildad, the Shuhite. Although the union was fruitful, Hebrew tradition has never allowed Keturah to take Sarah's place, as evidenced by the fact that in 1 Chronicles 1:32, Keturah is called a concubine. Another child born to this union was Midian; and, presumably, the Midianites are pictured as having sprung from him. However, in Judges 8:24, the Midianites are classed as Ishmaelites (cf. Gen. 37:25 ff.). There seems to be some confusion between the two groups, although it is possible that "Ishmaelites" became synonymous with the general term "Bedouin." Thus, the term "Ishmaelites" might represent the descendants of Ishmael, the child by Hagar, and yet, at the same time, be an all-inclusive term to include other groups.

His Death

Abraham's relationship to his friends and companions could be said to have been generally satisfactory. When the old man died at the age of one hundred and seventy-five years, a hundred of them having been spent in Canaan, there was little enmity, jealousy, or prejudice toward anyone. His house was in good order, and he apparently left none out of his concern. He left provisions for Isaac, for his sons by Keturah, and for the sons of his concubines.   Ishmael seems to have been satisfied with arrangements, for he attended the funeral.

Abraham's peaceful home-going is to be seen in the phrase "full of years" (25:8). He was satisfied with life. Upon his death, he was "gathered to his people" (25:8). Although the bulk of scholarship views such a phrase as meaning simply that one was buried in the family sepulcher, it cannot have that meaning here. The family sepulcher was back in Ur of the Chaldees or in Haran; thus, the phrase used here is inapplicable for such a faraway place. Skinner suggests that the concept of the family sepulcher is enlarged in its reference to Abraham and that it refers to the popular belief of that time that Abraham was gathered with the vast host of graves of the departed into the region of Sheol.[76]

However, at the risk of separation from the scholarly world, the present author would suggest that the early view of Keil and Delitzsch, which sees in the phrase some kind of hope in a continuation after this world, though ever so vague, is indicated.[77] Somewhat later, the same phrase is used of Jacob (49:33), and Jacob was in Egypt, much removed from any family sepulcher. To be sure, the expression "gathered to the fathers," or "to one's people," does not indicate any concept of either heaven or hell; but it does indicate existence beyond the grave in some vague fashion. Such a belief was a common concept of the people of Egypt and the Mesopotamian region, and it is less than logical to deny such a possibility here. Did those who worshiped the pagan gods have more hope than the adherents of the God of Abraham?

Thus was put to rest the one whom God called as the initiator of the covenant. Following him would be many who would continue in his train as instruments in bringing God's answer to the predicament of man. But all will be eternally

---

[76]Skinner, op. cit., p. 352.
[77]Keil and Delitzsch, op. cit., p. 263.

indebted to this man who demonstrated the meaning of faith in relation to a sovereign god of justice, mercy, and promise.

5. Man's Feebleness in God's Plan—Jacob (25:19 to 36:43)

Covenant Continuation in Isaac

A Needed Link

Even as suggested in the main heading for the chapter, most of this section of Genesis is concerned with the happenings of Jacob and his family. But Jacob can be understood better if some attempt is made to understand his father Isaac. It was really in Isaac that man's weakness in finding his place in God's redemptive purpose was most noticeable.

Something of Isaac's place in the larger pattern can be gathered from the fact that he is nearly always a background figure in the scene,[1] an accessory to the main act. He is presented in scenes of which either Abraham, Rebekah, or Jacob is the main personage. One of the most accurate things which can thus be said about him is that he was quiet, maybe too quiet, even lacking the basic self-assertion which would have prohibited his sometime use for improper purposes. Today he probably would be called mousy, simply because he did not make much noise. However, this deep quietness had something of meditation and devotion about it which set a pattern of commitment to God from which neither of his sons ever quite fully escaped. It must be remembered that to say a man is quiet and little inclined to self-assertion certainly does not say that he is bad. Some of the quiet ones are the deepest and most devoted ones. In this age of bombastic

---

[1]James Hastings (ed.), *The Greater Men and Women of the Bible* (Edinburgh: T. & T. Clark, 1913), I, 371.

performance and the selling of one's self, it might be well to remember that one of the characteristics of the messianic servant of the Lord was that he did "not cry nor lift up his voice, ... in the street" (Isa. 42:2, RSV). A man of such disposition was actually needed to tie together the *idealistic* Abraham and the *practical* Jacob. Isaac was the mediating point. His life provided a maturation period for the covenant idea to be understood and developed.

Some Positive Features

Among the positive characteristics in Isaac's character was his wholesome religion. One of the first appearances of Isaac in his adult life was in the meeting of his new bride. He had been out in the field for meditation (24:63). As some have suggested, it is possible that he was out there grieving over the loss of his mother. However, the word used to describe his action is *shuach,* which means basically to "sink down." Only in the *hiphil* stem does it indicate depression, such as mourning or grieving. Here it is in the *qal* stem and perhaps would indicate the kind of "sinking down" which comes from worship. A man of solitude, he was in the field for purer reflection with God.

More of the everyday piety in Isaac's life is to be seen in his prayer for a family. When his wife was barren, Isaac prayed to Yahweh for her (25:21). Every family which stemmed from Abraham was part of the covenant of God, so barrenness was a real handicap. Conscious of God's promise and of his ability to bless, Isaac prayed—certainly a fine trait for covenant extension.

The magnitude of this quality in Isaac's life did not appear until many years later. When his son Jacob, tired of the foreign country, reflected upon home and all for which home stood, he remembered his father, and his *father's religion* as the "fear of Isaac." The word used in 31:42 is *pachadh,* which is a verb basically meaning "to dread, be in dread, in awe, to have reverence." In Isaiah 60:5, with the subject "heart," it is translated, "Your heart shall thrill." As a noun it can mean awe, governor, or ruler. Thus, in spite of the treachery in which he himself engaged while living at home, Jacob thought of his father's home as a place where God was the ruler, before whom Isaac the father stood in awe.

Although certainly it is not a criterion for judging true religion, early Hebrews took long life and wealth of material blessing to be an indication of God's particular favor. Hebrew tradition felt it to be worth noting that Isaac lived longer than did the patriarchs Abraham and Jacob. Isaac died at one hundred and eighty years (35:28), Abraham at one hundred and seventy-five years (25:7), and Jacob at one hundred and forty-seven years (47:28). The content of Genesis 26:12-16 may be an indication that Isaac was also more prosperous than the other patriarchs. At least he did well enough to cause considerable comment. Hebrew tradition honored him as a man in favor with God.

Weaker Characteristics

Of course, the magnanimity of one phase of Isaac's life does not gloss out other aspects where more is to be desired. Some of these areas in which more might have been desired can be noted in Isaac's function as a son, husband, father, and as a neighbor.

As a son, Isaac's life was very definitely overshadowed by that of his great father. The favoritism, the overly protective attitude of Sarah, such as was seen in the Sarah-Hagar episode of chapter 21—all of this showed that Abraham and Sarah were so able and so willing to look after him that Isaac had little opportunity to develop his own initiative.

This subdued element in the son's life became even more evident when it came time for Isaac to prepare himself for the role of husband. Certainly Isaac was under the masterful personality of Abraham as plans were made to secure him a wife, but chapter 24:4 would indicate that he even acquiesced to Eliezer, the steward of Abraham; for Eliezer was far more active in securing a wife for Isaac than Isaac himself was. Isaac was forty years of age (25:20) when the marriage was arranged, and Rebekah was not brought to him on trial. According to 24:40,48,51, she was definitely being carried to Isaac as wife without any approval or disapproval on his part. This cannot be explained simply by saying that it was the custom of the day, for shortly thereafter Jacob had a great deal to say about whom he desired for a wife.

Perhaps a digression at this point will be permitted in order that there may be some glimpse of Rebekah, who was chosen as a wife for Isaac. She certainly was possessed of genuine beauty, for her first appearance before Eliezer was as a pure, unselfish, hard working but loving and lovable girl (24:16 ff.). It took Eliezer no time at all to decide that this one was that person upon whose nose he would place the gold ring (24:22, 47; cf. Isa. 3:21). Seemingly, she was a woman of decision; for even though marriage meant leaving home and family for a new destiny and destination, she made the decision to go. Apparently, those at home knew that she had a resolute will of her own, else they would never have asked her how she felt about the matter. Women of that day were not due such consideration under accepted custom.

As a father, Isaac seemed paternally negligent. Every evidence would indicate that he failed to try to work for amicable relations between his two sons. The actions of the two boys would indicate that the father had not been diligent in executing his responsibilities as preserver of the covenant. Finally, Esau married a Canaanite. Maybe Isaac had not exercised enough control. Certainly Abraham would never have allowed Isaac to marry a Canaanite. This may indicate that Isaac was so lenient with his son that he felt his better judgment slip. It would appear that he thought it better to allow Esau to have his own way without regard to an insistence that he marry a woman of his own faith so as to perpetuate the covenant.

The birthright episode was an additional indication that Isaac had little discipline over his household—a sad commentary on his own weakness. Isaac demonstrated emotional instability when in premature fashion he called Esau for the purpose of blessing him, for Isaac lived on eighty years more. Isaac simply became panicky and wanted to give his favorite the blessing. The skirmish between Jacob and Esau disturbed Isaac, and so he initiated the idea of giving the blessing early rather than waiting until immediately prior to his death, as was the normal custom (cf. Gen. 49). A look at the chronology will indicate the hastiness of his action. Isaac was sixty years of age when the twins were born (25:26); at the age of one hundred, supposedly on his death bed, he blessed Jacob (26:34; 27:24). Yet Isaac lived until he was one hundred and eighty years of age (35:28).

The neighbors of Isaac evidently recognized his weakness also. As long as Abraham lived, there was no molestation of the wells belonging to the Hebrews. However, after Abraham's death the people of the land began to encroach upon Isaac's rights and evidently stopped the wells by filling them with stones (26:15,18), a practice frequently resorted to in desert warfare. Isaac easily was driven about from one well to another. It was only when pushed to the limit at Beersheba (26:27) that he dared assert himself for the purpose of honoring his father's memory at the old wells and to claim his rights as his father's heir, and, consequently, as father and preserver of the covenant.

It is interesting that not until after Isaac asserted himself did he receive any genuine assurance about the covenant. Did he have to prove himself worthy to be a covenant bearer? Perhaps this experience helped to strengthen Isaac, for he immediately built an altar (26:25). Although weak, God strengthened him for the keeping of the covenant purposes.

Covenant Continuation in Jacob

Amply illustrated in Abraham's concern for Isaac was the truth of the axiom that "if the people of God are to have a history, then what one generation does for the next is important." The same concern was not evidenced by Isaac, and the lack of it became apparent in the life of Jacob.

Life at Home with Esau (25:19-34; 27:1-45)

Background (25:19-28).—The comment of 25:33, indicative of continual strife between the people of Jacob and Esau, is perhaps a reflection, based on fact, by the Priestly writer of a later age. At any rate, it certainly reflects a contrast which was true from the very beginning. The rift was in embryo stage when Jacob developed tendencies which kept him close to the house, while Esau developed those which kept him out-of-doors. Isaac, although a quiet man, apparently had great admiration for the outdoor life. He went there for meditation (24:63), and he loved its smell and fresh atmosphere (27:27). Though Esau seems to have enjoyed nature because of its rougher aspects, there is between Isaac and Esau this kindred appreciation for God's world. It was only natural that the two should be closely drawn together.

However, with this alignment, there was of course the danger of family division, a fact which makes a bit more understandable the constant scheming of Rebekah and Jacob. With a word, an old patriarch could control destiny, and with Isaac's close attachment to Esau, it looked as though Jacob might be left out altogether.

Thus, perhaps because Esau represented the kind of natural manhood which he himself failed to be, Isaac favored Esau; and, because Jacob possessed some finer cultural qualities which naturally appeal to women, Rebekah favored him. Although the *American Book of Common Prayer* mentions Isaac and Rebekah as being the only pair of patriarchs who seem

to have been monogamous, there was much about the home
to sow discord.

Esau's native characteristics and his use of them may serve
as an indicator as to God's apparent preference for Jacob.
Although Esau may have had no intention of doing evil, he
was too preoccupied to be bothered with God. Being a hunter,
he never got around to doing what he ought to do; lacking
discipline, he followed his impulses. On the other hand, Jacob
although with many faults, had underneath a current which
Esau did not have. He was a "quiet" man (25:27). The term
is *tam,* which means "complete, perfect in basic purpose or
nature." As can be seen by the use of the word with reference
to Noah and Job, it indicates that a man was at least "searching" after God. Jacob was in control of himself, whereas Esau
lacked self-discipline.

Groundwork for tension (25:29-32).—In considering the
rift which finally erupted between Jacob and Esau, it must be
remembered that Isaac and Rebekah actually had little to do
with the original breach between the two boys.

Esau was the careless type who failed to weigh values. Like
little children living on any street who will sacrifice or trade
things of great value to satisfy immediate whims, so Esau was
ready to follow his impulses without careful calculation. He
was willing to trade the treasure of the permanent, his covenant responsibility, for the immediacy of the temporary. The
ready willingness to sacrifice such a remote good shows the
profane nature that characterized him. This weakness on the
part of Esau does not mean that one can justify Jacob, but it
does help to understand him.

Of course, it was the birthright which lay at the center of
the controversy (25:31). The very fact that Jacob immediately asked for the birthright may be an indication that he
had been smarting under what he felt to be unequal treatment.
To understand this is to understand the significance of birthright. Used just seven times in the Old Testament, the term

bekhorah denotes the rights and privileges normally enjoyed by the elder son. Sometime ago there appeared on a national television program a contestant from Africa who bore six tribal marks on his face. These tribal marks were testimony that he was an elder son and that he had certain rights. The custom embodies the type of situation involved in the Old Testament "birthright."

It was thought that the oldest son possessed a natural vigor of body and character which made success in life inevitable (Gen. 49:3; Deut. 21:17). Furthermore, he was to occupy a position of honor as head of the family (27:29; 49:8), and to him belonged a double share of the inheritance (Deut. 21: 15 ff.). All of this culminated in the elder son's responsibility as spiritual head of the family, through whom the covenant responsibility was to be transmitted.

Something seriously wrong is apparent in the life of Esau for him to part so willingly with his privileges and responsibilities. The indication here is that he did not care about the covenant. In 1 Chronicles 5:1 f. there is an indication that the birthright could be transferred legally from the actual first-born son to another who proved more worthy of the dignity. The entire setting of the story emphasizes that Esau was *not* worthy, and Genesis 25:34 gives some justification that if Esau were defrauded, he was defrauded of that which he was incapable of appreciating.

Jacob apparently wanted the spiritual blessing, as well as the prosperity. His mistake was not in wanting the spiritual, but in the manner in which he got it. Indeed, his later willingness to work twenty years indicates that the spiritual phase of the blessing may have been his main concern. However, the end did not justify the means.

The breach (27).—Tension was increased to the breaking point when Jacob procured his father's blessing by a fraud. Evidently, Isaac thought he was dying, and so he purposed to bestow a dying wish upon Esau (27:4). The universal belief in the efficacy of a dying wish appears often in the Old Testament.[2] Apparently, it was felt that the total *nephesh,* or inner being of an individual, gathered up all of its force in a single potent and prophetic wish which thus so set events in motion that they came to pass.

The oral blessing was in the nature of both a religious and a material testament, and, of course, in this instance, much was involved; for certainly there was some word of concern about leadership in the covenant. It was believed that such an oracle, once spoken, was inevitable (27:33 f.). Thus, Esau did not hope for the blessing to be reversed; he only asked for a second, even though inferior blessing. The Nuzi tablets, which reflect customs known in patriarchal society, indicate that such irrevocable oral blessings were upheld in court.

Evidently the blessing was connected with eating (27:4), and the question arises as to why. Skinner, building somewhat upon the thought of Gunkel, suggests that the food served as the physical stimulus which was often needed to induce prophetic inspiration.[3] Furthermore, in addition to insuring the general pleasantness of the situation and making it more memorable, the meal may have been something of a sacrificial meal, thus establishing communion with deity. If this last element were involved, then it would have been a striking part of Isaac's blessing, for it would have involved Yahweh as a witness to the covenant transmission. Evidence that it was, in this case, largely a religious ceremony is enhanced by the suggestion that best clothes were demanded for the occasion (27:15).

Although Esau had been quite willing at an earlier period to sell his birthright for a bowl of pottage, or as the word *'adhashim* implies, dried bean soup, when it finally dawned upon him that this would lead to relinquishing the blessing,

---

[2]Cf. Gen. 48:10 ff.; 50:24 f.; Deut. 33; Josh. 23; 2 Sam. 23:1 f.; 1 Kings 2:1 ff.; 2 Kings 13:14 ff.

[3]Skinner, *op. cit.,* p. 369 f. Cf. also 1 Sam. 10:5 f.; 2 Kings 3:15.

he was like a trapped and hurt animal (27:38) and begged for some kind of blessing. In him is seen the way of a man who fails to consider the consequences of his deeds. How often man fails to realize how valuable something is until it is lost! It was too much for poor Esau, and under the heat of the moment, he purposed revenge (27:41-45). Esau later mellowed but his descendants never did. What a plight for those who were supposed to be part of a covenant of love—but now a covenant of hate.

Life Away from Home (*28-36*)

Flight and encounter (*28:1-22*).—It was more than the need of a wife which sent Jacob from the locale of Beer-sheba to a distant place. Such a deed as his not only caused difficult relations with a deceived brother, from whom Jacob had much to fear, but the experience left him with a burdened conscience, which he would seek to cover with the business of travel. However, a stricken conscience cannot be escaped, especially when one tries to sleep. Perhaps the many thoughts on his troubled soul provided the crisis, which, upon his arrival at Bethel, resulted in his audience with deity.

With a disturbed inner experience, he lay down for sleep when, half between the conscious and the subconscious, he dreamed of a ladder set up between heaven and earth with angels ascending and descending on it (28:11-12). This was God's way of revealing himself to a lonely wanderer. The term "ladder" simply indicates "something elevated." It could have been suggested from a nearby hillside cut with steps. At any rate, it served as a symbol to indicate that there can be an approach to God, even by a wayward wanderer such as Jacob. Lonesome and having reflected on his sin, Jacob previously may have reached the conclusion that there was no hope of his ever really mending his relationship with God. Perhaps he had brooded over a feeling of having actually lost the position of being able to serve as an instrument of the covenant because of his flight from home. Now, in a dramatic way, God has broken into the history of his life.

Though the picture of the angels ascending and descending might at first seem to be a reversed expression, it is not, for the picture is that of the transmission of Jacob's thoughts and requests to God and the bringing back an answer. A blessing is promised Jacob by Yahweh, who stood close to Jacob. The Hebrew is ambiguous and can be translated either as placing the Lord above the top of the ladder or beside Jacob. At any rate, the intended emphasis is the same. God appeared in personal fashion to Jacob; in addition to bringing assurance of personal care and concern, the Lord renewed for Jacob the promise which he had made already for Abraham and Isaac.

The content of verse 13 confirms Jacob as covenant leader, in spite of his many weak tendencies. This in no sense indicates God's approval upon Jacob's method in obtaining the responsibility of leadership. Some express surprise that Yahweh did not outwardly condemn Jacob because of his sin. However, no spoken condemnation was necessary. Simply for Jacob to be in God's presence was condemnation enough, to say nothing of the littleness Jacob must have felt in God's allowing him to carry on the covenant.

It is a serious thing to bear the covenant responsibility. This realization of responsibility, coupled with the graphic nature of his immediate experience, led Jacob to exclaim, "The Lord is in this place" (28:16). Here was God's unexpected presence.

As someone has suggested, the earthly sanctuary which Jacob built became the entrance to heaven. His immediate reaction was fear rather than joy. After all, initially, he had treated this holy place on which he stood as common ground. Such a confrontation left him with uneasiness (28:17). Surely his experience is evidence that there is legitimacy in fear in religion. Reverence and dread were the root of his realization of previous failure. This experience, though at times forgotten, was something of a turning point in Jacob's life. That which has been commonplace to him was now holy (28:18), and the locale should henceforth have a new name. It was no longer to be what men called it but what God *made* it (28:19).

Following such an experience, one would expect to find a vow, dedication, and commitment to the covenant task; and he does. The vow of verse 20 is introduced with an "if," which is often misunderstood. In *if* clauses in the Hebrew language, introduced by *'im, if* as here, the usual method of implying a condition which might embody some doubt is to combine "if" with verbs in the so-called imperfect state, both in the protasis and in the apodosis.[4] However, when the condition is expressed in the mind with a certain realization that it will come to pass, the Hebrew perfect is used.[5] In this instance in verse 20, there occurs a perfect in both the protasis and apodosis. Therefore, Jacob was really saying, "If the Lord can keep on working with a scoundrel like me, and he can, then I *shall* do certain things." The reason the vow expressed so strongly the idea of getting back home was his realization that the covenant was primarily connected, not with Mesopotamia, but with the land of Canaan. Jacob did not make a cheap bargain with God.

Forgotten vows and difficult times (29-31).—This phase of the life of Jacob in a pagan environment is quite similar to the experience of Abraham, who, after his covenant commitment, let fear of famine cause him to forget his vow and enter into treacherous deceit in Egypt. To be sure, this does not excuse Jacob, but it does aid in understanding him. Jacob's tendencies were like those of every man—allowing a startling and gripping experience in life to be followed by spiritual relaxation and forgetfulness.

These tendencies of Jacob were certainly encouraged while

---

[4] A. B. Davidson, *Hebrew Syntax* (3rd ed.; Edinburgh: T. & T. Clark, 1912), p. 175.

[5] *Ibid.*, p. 176.

he was with Laban's family. His very human side, interestingly, is presented in his introduction to the family through his meeting with Rachel. When he first saw Rachel, he suggested to the shepherds who were hanging around that they ought to go ahead and take care of their work; in essence he wanted to be alone with Rachel (29:7). Jacob was so excited that when he saw this good-looking girl, he felt a certain burst of strength and removed the heavy wellstone by himself (29:10).

Laban's initial acceptance of Jacob (29:14) was quite cordial. The phrase "my bone and my flesh" elsewhere implies a very intimate or even legal relationship.[6] In this setting, the phrase seems to serve as a formal recognition of the ties of friendship between them, indicative both of formal greeting and friendship. Jacob was received as part of the family.

From succeeding events it is evident that Laban's attitude later changed. There are those who feel that much time elapsed between verses 14 and 15 of chapter 29 and that the change in attitude came during that period. Daube and Yaron, of Oxford, who have spent much energy on a study of ancient law, suggest that the question about wages in verse 15 is really a question which renounced Jacob as a brother and that the offering of wages was a degradation of Jacob's status, thus excluding Jacob from the family relationship.[7] The question bears need of further study in connection with the final defection between Laban and Jacob.

True love takes little account of time, and Jacob himself suggested that he serve seven years for Rachel (29:18). Deception in connection with the marriage was possible because of the custom of the bride's being veiled as she was brought to the bridegroom. Perhaps this can be considered as part of the law of retribution; Jacob deceived and was deceived in return

---

[6]Gen. 2:23; Judg. 9:2; 2 Sam. 5:1; 19:13; 1 Chron. 11:1.
[7]David Daube and Reuven Yaron, "Jacob's Reception by Laban," *The Journal of Semitic Studies*, I (January, 1956), 60-62.

(29:23). Laban had some legitimate cause for his action, according to the custom of his times (29:26). The objection to giving a younger daughter before an older was natural and prevails in some countries today.

Perhaps the most sordid part of Jacob's entire career is to be seen in the births of his children. He was a pawn in the hand of scheming women. In spite of much attention given to Rachel, ultimately Jacob seems to have had more lasting appreciation for Leah, for it was Leah whom he chose to honor by burial in the family sepulcher at Machpelah (chap. 49). Perhaps the passage of the years aided Jacob in better evaluating the two women.

In the fight between Rachel and Leah to have the honor of childbirth, further allusion is made to the primitive ceremony of adoption, already mentioned in connection with the struggle between Sarah and Hagar, a ceremony in which the child of the handmaiden was actually brought forth on the knees of the adopted mother (30:3). The desperateness of the struggle is to be seen in the fight for mandrakes (30:14). The mandrake was a round, greenish-yellow, plum-like fruit, which in Syria ripens in May and is still sought in the East to promote conception. Although clearly a superstition, the fruit was thought to be efficacious in facilitating conception.

The difficulty involved in the apparent forgetting of the Bethel vow is further intensified in Jacob's rift with Laban. Even the agreed settlement that Jacob should take the speckled and off-colored of the flock was filled with deception (30: 25-43). The partly colored animals were few, for the Syrian sheep were generally all white and the goats were either brown or black. Laban, who apparently had not been too well blessed before (30:27), took some of these which were to have been Jacob's and slipped them into his son's flocks. When one forgets his covenant vow, he feels the necessity of survival through deceptive and self-reliant measures, and Jacob ran true to form. Motivated by a common superstition, he took tree boughs, pulled strips of bark from them, placed them in front of the places where the flocks came to drink and thought that, in his smartness, he had enriched himself (30:37). However, the intended emphasis is that any blessing which came came through God's providence and not through Jacob's ingenuity (31:5,7,9,11,13).

Certainly the "shady" practices of Jacob did nothing to lessen his tension with Laban, and so, shrewdly, he and his family slipped away. Both Jacob and Laban seized upon imperfections in their dealing with each other to rationalize individually their actions. Laban had deceived Jacob in the matter of wages; and, apparently, he had also broken the ancient custom of giving the *mohar,* the wedding price paid by the groom to the bride, keeping it instead and using it selfishly on himself (31:15). Jacob and his family were indignant. On the other hand, Laban was incensed, probably feeling that these younger people had broken the control which he, as a patriarchal father, had a right to exercise over the patriarchal family. Anger was intensified upon his discovery that Rachel and Jacob had stolen the teraphim, household gods, (31:19). The only thing which archaeologists have found which could be equated to the household gods are figurines or small statues of goddesses. Apparently, possession of the household gods was thought to secure family life, and evidently their possession gave legal title to the family's property.[8] Is it any wonder that Laban was disturbed?

Contrary to what might have been expected, peace ultimately resulted between Laban and Jacob, but the Scripture writer would remind the reader that it was no accident. God's providence was active in preserving from harm this appointed bearer of the covenant faith (31:29). Thus, in spite of the enmity between the two, peace was possible because God had spoken. Once again Jacob was reduced to a shaking admission

[8]Cyrus H. Gordon, *The World of the Old Testament* (Garden City: Doubleday & Co., Inc., 1958), p. 129.

of God's help and with it made an agreement with Laban, which was a pledge both to Laban and to God (31:44). Jacob suggested that to break the agreement which they were making would be tantamount to breaking a vow with God (31: 49-50). Since God was a witness to the agreements between the men, their agreement was in essence a pledge to God.

In the passage which has been immediately before us there is apparent evidence that the present form of the Jacob story was composed from earlier sources. Remnants of both sources are allowed to remain for the sake of emphasis. Two names are explained (Galeed and Mizpah, 48*b*-49*a*), and two sacred monuments were erected. One is called a heap of stones (cairn, 46,48,51-52), while the other is called a pillar (monolith, 49,51-52). Twice the covenant feast is recorded (46*b*,54), and the terms of the covenant are given in two forms, with God being twice called to witness (49-53).

Heightening of religious experience (*32-36*).—**32:1-21.** Embodied in the first twenty-one verses of this section is an entreaty to rely on God. Jacob separated from his father-in-law Laban and continued on his way with a realization that a genuine test lay ahead of him—the meeting with Esau. It was while turning this matter over in his mind that the "angels of God met him" (32:1). The word translated "met," *way yiph ge'u,* is from a root which means "to meet in the sense of oppose" or "to inflict pain" and, consequently, "to encounter with the purpose of request or entreaty." The last suggested use of the word occurs in Jeremiah 7:16 and in Job 21:15. Thus, this appearance was for the purpose of afflicting inward spiritual pain and a consequent entreaty to rely on God. Through this experience, Jacob was stimulated into a reminder that he traveled not just with his army but with God's hosts, so he named the place of the experience *Mahanaim,* "two armies." It was his realization of the traveling presence of God.

Jacob's subsequent actions in the chapter suggest to many that the Mahanaim experience was wrapped in the shallow blanket of religious emotion and that Jacob forgot it immediately upon having to meet Esau. However, such is not likely.

Upon hearing of the strength of Esau (v. 6), Jacob realized more than before that he himself had a great deal to do. God helps those who help themselves. The difficulty in which he found himself made him realize more than ever that his only hope of deliverance and safety was with God's blessing (v. 9), and he seemed to have in view God's wider purpose of covenant performance (v. 12). His covenant commitment was expressed in a beautiful prayer containing the elements of invocation (v. 9), thanksgiving (v. 10), petition (v. 11), and reliance upon divine faithfulness (v. 12).

32:22 to 33:20. This section deals with a character-changing experience (Peniel). The tension between brothers, the long separation, the dangers involved—all of these things brought great heaviness to the mind and heart of Jacob.

After securing his group for the night, Jacob himself lay down, only to have a long, restless, struggling night. Who was the wrestler who came in the darkness of the night, the common time for attacks of spiritual anxiety? Is it possible that this is a literary vehicle for showing Jacob's inward struggle with God? Is this an Old Testament dramatization of the consequence that comes to every soul which has tried too long to evade the truth about itself?

The phrase in verse 26, "Let me go, for the day is breaking," gives rise to the suggestion that the literary form used here exhibits a survival of the ancient belief in night spirits which roamed at night and vanished at dawn, a superstition still known in Shakespeare's day.[9]

Frazer directs attention to the ancient belief that rivers had personal features and resented being crossed and suggests that involved in the Genesis passage is the remnant of an ancient belief that there was a deity (spirit) which protected the

---

[9] Cf. *Hamlet*, Act I, scene 1.

Jabbok River and that the author's acquaintance with this belief led him to use the old superstition as a framework for reporting Jacob's spiritual experience.[10] The Hebrew root for Jabbok is *yavak*, "to empty," and the root of "wrestle" is *'avak*, whose primary meaning is "run."[11] When the root is used in noun form, it means "dust"; such is stirred up when one runs. "Wrestle" is an infrequent meaning for the word. Does the author use it just to make a play on words with Jabbok? Does it indicate that this was a struggle which shook Jacob so that he "rolled in the dust?"

Though the literary framework suggested above determined the pattern in which the material is presented to us, the emphasis in the passage is that of the triumph of spiritual religion, showing that, regardless of how it comes, God often uses man's frustrations as a basis for a struggling spiritual experience, and, taking advantage of man's darkness, speaks to him in the quiet and terror of the night.

Some indication that the wrestling should not be taken as a literal experience is to be found in Hosea 12:4, which indicates that Jacob strove with an *angel* and prevailed, whereas Genesis 32:28 says he strove with God. That the phrase "For I have seen God face to face" (32:30) is an interpretation of a spiritual experience is counter-balanced from being "physical" by such a passage as Exodus 33:20, which reads, " 'you cannot see my face; for man shall not see me and live.' "

The eternal principle of the passage and the message for our day is that, in the hour of despair and struggle, Jacob continued to talk with God until he got some help. In this sense, man can have direct contact with God. It is no wonder that he remembered the place as Peniel, the face of God. His had been the kind of spiritual experience which Job later had also when he cried out, "I had heard of thee by the hearing of the ear, but now mine eye seeth thee" (Job. 42:5). Thus, one sees

---

[10]Frazer, *op. cit.*, p. 419 f.
[11]Skinner, *op. cit.*, p. 411.

the significance in the change of his own name from Jacob (supplanter) to Israel (he who strives with God).

On the strength of such an experience, Israel (Jacob) was able to meet Esau with good spirit, and in gracious fashion bowed before him seven times. In the pattern of the ancient East, sevenfold prostration (33:7) was a formula indicative of genuine respect and good will. The providence of God had prepared Jacob for a healing experience with Esau. However, seed of strife already sown could not be erased, and their differences remained in their descendants for generations. So much had happened to facilitate his return that Jacob went on to Shechem and settled down. That he had had a new and determined purpose is indicated in the name which he called the place of his altar, *El Elohe Israel*, God the God of Israel. In his own mind, there was no doubt about it; this was his personal God who had brought him through.

34. The sordid events of chapter 34 indicate a spiritual relapse on the part of Jacob. They are followed by a time of fresh commitment to God (chap. 35). Just how much time passed it is impossible to tell, but, true to his previously observed nature, Jacob seems to have lost the initial spark from some of the great experiences which he had and had allowed his spiritual ambition to smolder in the everyday affairs of life.

Relaxation of religious concern was reflected in wayward sons and daughters, the culmination of which was the desecration of Dinah, Jacob's daughter, by a heathen prince (34:2). A compromise solution was reached under Jacob's leadership and, externally and superficially, Hamor's people became covenant people through wholesale circumcision (34:15), an ancient emphasis upon the externality of religion very similar to the incident tens of centuries later when Constantine marched his troops into the sea in a wholesale, forced baptism. But nothing ever really helps unless it has touched the mainspring of a people's heart. Thus, trouble flared again, and Levi and Simeon took the sword and mutilated many Shechemites.

Perhaps involved here is an indication that Jacob, even with all of God's help, had taken the covenant responsibility to be primarily an external one. The very fact that the sons immediately thought about the necessity of circumcising the Shechemites, if they were to live together, is an indication that the spiritual nature of the covenant had not been fully understood.

Here then in the life of one of the patriarchs is a preview of what was to happen later. The people named after the "man" Israel had also to suffer because they, like Jacob in this instance, were happy to accept the blessings without realization of the responsibilities involved. In verse 12 of chapter 32 there is no indication of a remembrance that his blessings were for others.

As failure to comprehend the spiritual nature of the covenant led later Israel into exile, so Jacob's shortcomings resulted in fear and withdrawal (34:30). Certainly here is further emphasis that "to whom much is given much is required."

35. God in his grace, however, has a way of pointing out to man the gap between him and God, and, in turn, of bridging that gap.[12] Erelong Jacob saw the necessity, physically and spiritually, of re-treading the way to Bethel. God has a way of taking advantage of man's heartaches and using them for a purpose, and so the experience relative to Dinah became a reminder to Jacob of his vow at Bethel. It was not just a superstitious idea. By returning Jacob hoped to recapture something of the atmosphere and dynamic of the original Bethel experience.

Realizing that much of the preparation for a spiritual pilgrimage must be his, Jacob had those under his influence to turn in their idols and earrings. The fact that it was necessary to call for the idols gives some indication of their religious need. The earrings were objects of superstition and were generally associated with false worship (cf. Hos. 2:13). In

---

[12]Karl Barth, *The Epistle to the Romans,* trans. Edwyn C. Hoskyns (London: Oxford University Press, 1933), p. 31.

spite of the turmoil of the environment and in spite of what had been done to the Shechemites, none pursued. Jacob and all that were with him traveled under the protection of God (35:5), as man always does when he makes an effort to go back to God.

The resultant profit of the trip was a profound and personal experience for Jacob. Before, the picture was always that of God's seeking Jacob. Now Jacob seeks God and is rewarded by a fresh and dynamic personal experience (35:9 ff.).

But it was an experience sealed with sorrow, for Rachel died on the trip. Yet, even this was punctuated with joy, for Rachel's death meant the birth of Benjamin. It had been a long journey, but all of the experiences were climaxed with a reconciliation at his father Isaac's home (35:27). Jacob had been humbled and buffeted and was now repentant and could carry out his covenant responsibility. As a transformed man, he was prepared at last to bear the transforming message.

36. Chapter 36 is an exceedingly difficult chapter. It seems to be placed here for the purpose of summarizing Esau's line as of secondary importance in order to remove him from the scene as a preface to the further development of Jacob's line with a study of its turmoil in Egypt. Since Esau departed from Canaan (36:6), it is apparent that Esau recognized the covenant leadership on Canaanite soil as now belonging to Jacob.

Various glimpses in the material are of interest. The name Eliphaz, mentioned in the genealogy of the chapter, is mentioned again only in Job 2:11, where one by this name appears as the wisest friend of Job. The mention of the Edomite kings in the chapter would suggest that Edom attained a political organization much sooner than did Israel, perhaps some 150 to 200 years prior to David. Verses 31-39 would indicate that the early kingship was not hereditary since no king presented here is the son of a predecessor. Probably these early kings were more like the early judges of Israel, who, during their lifetime, ruled as local chieftains but were never able to consolidate their gains and establish a dynasty.

Perhaps it is proper to conclude this larger section on the "heightening of religious experience," chapters 32-36, with the suggestion that in Jacob the reader views a man who wanted, down deep, to be obedient but, because of his fleshly nature, had a hard time doing so.   God, however, did not cast him aside.   Instead, he patiently worked with him until he won Jacob and prepared Jacob to transmit spiritual heritage.   From God's experience with Jacob, we should learn that we cannot judge men from God's perspective.   We may often be mistaken in consigning a man to hopelessness.

6. God's Perseverance in His Plan—Joseph (37-50)

Nature of the Material

S. H. Hooke has been of much help in formulating an approach to the Joseph stories as compared with other patriarchal material.[1]   Whereas, the material with reference to Abraham, Isaac, and Jacob was presented in loose and disconnected narratives, the Joseph material is a single and connected romance with a dramatic development.   Whereas, in the Abraham to Jacob narratives, God constantly appears and directly intervenes in the actual course of events, in the Joseph material there is presented an emphasis upon the remote hand of sovereign providence, often intervening in Joseph's behalf but seldom making an appearance in personal fashion.   While other parts of Genesis have a cultic interest in shrines and altars, this is of little importance in the last section of the book.

Someone has called the material a "novelistic" narrative, for it unfolds an interesting plot with the presentation of challeng-

---

[1]Cf. Hooke, *The Siege Perilous,* pp. 173-183.

ing conflict between character and circumstance. Its chief character, Joseph, is not the paragon of merely one virtue but of many. He is the ideal son, brother, servant, and administrator. Material from individual biography and tribal history has been woven together by the biblical writer to present a charming picture.

Many scholars have tried to ferret out the historical background of the Joseph stories with a view toward ascertaining how much of the narrative may be understood as literal history. Certainly there are elements suggesting folklore. For instance, the account of Joseph's temptation by Potiphar's wife is so closely paralleled by an Egyptian story known as *The Tale of Two Brothers* that the parallel can hardly be accidental.

A historical critique of the Joseph stories is made more difficult because of the lack of proper names. There are four proper names used—Potiphar (39:1); Potiphera, priest of On (41:45); Asenath, daughter of the priest (41:45); and the name Zaphenath-peneah (41:45), which Joseph was given upon his elevation to the office of prime minister. Egyptologists suggest that these are names which linguistically indicate a period in the twenty-first or twenty-second Egyptian dynasties, or about 1200-1000 B.C. Although the form of the names does not indicate the date of the material, it does indicate the approximate period by which the literary form of the stories had reached a stable and fixed status.

Little help is to be found in a study of place names, for only two appear. These are the "land of Rameses" (47:11), the dwelling place of the Israelites, and "the land of Goshen," apparently, a synonymous phrase. Goshen was the region in the eastern part of the Nile Delta. Some papyri from the nineteenth Egyptian dynasty indicate that at times Bedouins from the Sinai Peninsula were allowed to pasture their flocks in the Goshen district, a custom which supported the Hebrews there (47:4-6). The phrase "land of Rameses" is apparently an anachronism and offers little help, for the strength of Rameses was not in existence until the nineteenth dynasty, a period too late to provide the setting for the Joseph material.

Thus, Hooke is right in suggesting that though the Genesis narrator presents a true Egyptian portrayal, he does it according to the life and custom of his own age and offers little contemporary help in ascertaining the age of the Joseph family.[2]

The most prominent historical clue in the entire narrative is the mention of the chariot (41:43). Since the chariot, along with the horse, was introduced into Egyptian life by the Hyksos (1710-1550), the passage must date from the Hyksos period or later. Of course, to mention the Hyksos is to arouse the very difficult question of their identity, a problem far too lengthy for detailed investigation here. Suffice it to say, however, that the term "Hyksos" seems to imply something like "rulers of foreign lands," perhaps a designation which the native Egyptians gave when a mixed group took over the Delta and upper Egypt region *ca.* 1700 B.C. Some of the Hyksos were of Semitic stock, so their invasion of the country would provide a natural setting for the reception of Joseph and his family.

But help at this point causes a problem at another. The Hyksos worshiped their god, Set, and tried to stifle the influence of Ra, the sun god, ordinarily the chief deity of Egypt with a main temple situated at On (Heliopolis). Hooke suggests that this raises the dual problem of the permission of sun worship by the Hyksos, with temple and priestly status, as well as the problem of a prime minister's marriage to the daughter of a priest of an outlawed religion.

However, the problem is not as serious as it might seem. Since the Hyksos were a mixed multitude, it is entirely possible that multiple religion was in some sense allowed. There are two additional possibilities. The forced giving of a displaced

---

[2]Cf. Hooke, *In the Beginning.* pp. 113-120.

priest's daughter to a non-Egyptian and one of a foreign religion may have served as a means of humiliating former sun worshipers, thus helping to accomplish the Hyksos purpose. Furthermore, it is entirely possible that the Hyksos had taken over a former temple of Ra and were using it for Set. This too would have degraded sun worship.

It requires an attempt at too much reading between the lines to give a complete picture of the nature of this material. It is enough to say that it reflects the historical and cultural flavoring of Egypt with sufficiently heightened and dramatic intensification to serve as a worthy vehicle for emphasis upon the religious truth of God's providence in the presentation and perpetuation of his covenant people.

In the story are some scattered remnants of the Priestly source, but most of the material is to be attributed to J and E. The two prominent sources are more easily identified by the switch in the names Israel (J) and Jacob (E) for the old patriarch than by variation in the divine name. Yahweh is prominent in chapter 39, but elsewhere Elohim holds the stage.

Thus, here begins a long body of material, all of which is concerned immediately with Joseph except the story of Judah and Tamar, which is included as an interruption in chapter 38, and the blessing of Jacob, which serves as something of a summary appendix in chapter 49 and must be considered separately.

It is the simple story of God's providential hand in the growth of a family of people into a nation. Here is a portrait which assures in no uncertain terms that this plan of redemption is God's from beginning to end. Such is demonstrated through the lives of those with whom God is dealing. A parallel theme is the helpfulness of the Chosen People, God's instruments, to those even outside of Israel; Joseph saved Egypt from famine. The device which he used to ward off its worst effects is illustrated by Egyptian inscriptions.

Joseph's Solitary Career in Egypt (37; 39-41)

The Preparation of Joseph Through Severe Trial (37; 39)

The trial of family enmity (37).—One will have to say that Joseph's solitary career in Egypt, made necessary because of his brothers' betrayal, was somewhat his own doing. It was almost inevitable that the alienation from his brothers should happen.

Joseph himself prepared the way by bringing an evil report (37:2), by allowing himself to bask in the favoritism of Jacob (37:3), and by his frank description of his dreams (37:5-9). Someone has suggested that in his actions are the three easy lessons for developing trouble. To be perfectly and tactlessly frank with others, to allow one's self to be given honors above others, to visualize dreams and opportunities ahead of others —here is the pathway to privilege but also to heartache. Joseph could have averted some of the hatred, but, instead, he increased it by relating everything which happened to him.

The father's favoritism and contribution to the tension is pictured in his gift of the "coat of extremities." The Revised Standard Version translation as "a long robe with sleeves" is far more accurate than the King James' "coat of many colors." The Hebrew has no reference to colors but implies a type of coat which indicated administrative or white collar work. An ordinary garment was sleeveless and reached only to the knees. That it was an unusual garment can be gathered from its use by the daughters of kings in 2 Samuel 13:18 ff. By the bestowal of this garment and the corresponding honor, Jacob did what he pleased without regard to the feelings of his other sons. Joseph seems to have done his utmost to capitalize upon the fact.

It was only natural that Jacob should be concerned about the other sons when they tarried long with their flocks, for they were in the vicinity of Shechem, the place where Dinah had been molested and where the men previously had gotten into trouble (cf. chap. 34). When Joseph was sent to look for them, his inexperienced and protected existence was soon evident. A debt of gratitude is owed the unnamed man who found him (37:15).

The drama was intensified as the brothers saw Joseph approaching. Their reference to him as "the dreamer" (37:19) was a mocking epithet which evidenced their enmity. Neither the concerned Reuben (37:22) nor the hesitant Judah (37:26) was strong enough to curb the fruit of this enmity, and Joseph was carried into Egypt.

Admittedly, there is difficulty in the story here, for the J and E sources do not seem to have been conflated as smoothly as they might have been. In one instance the Ishmaelites took Joseph (37:27), and in another instance he was taken by the Midianites (37:28). Several attempted answers have been given. It has been suggested that the Midianites first bought him and then sold him to the Ishmaelites, a separate group of people. However, the context would seem to indicate that the Midianites and the Ishmaelites were the same. The Midianites were descendants of Abraham by Keturah (Gen. 25), while the Ishmaelites were descendants of Abraham by Hagar (Gen. 16). Thus, the two groups could be referred to as one with their names used interchangeably. The difference in names is because of a particular preference for the one name or the other by the locales which gave rise to the two sources.

The enmity was highlighted by its ultimate deception of Jacob the father. Perhaps the dipping of Joseph's coat into goat blood is related by the author for the purpose of reminding the reader of that time when Jacob deceived his father by killing a he-goat and seeking a blessing. This is the harvest of a deceptive seed sown ever so many years before.

Much of the suffering of Jacob's old age was due to the sin of his youth. The little interlude of attention to Jacob is redirected with the final notation of the chapter that Joseph reached Egypt and was sold into the household servitude of

Potiphar, the "captain of the guards," or as the Hebrew seems to imply, the "chief of the executions." The one who had dreamed of grandeur thus found himself tried in the status of a slave.

The trial of sensual pleasure (*39:1-19*).—In spite of the fact that Joseph was far from home in the midst of the lax moral life of Egypt, he was able to withstand the test. Strength was his, for he somehow had been able to maintain a consciousness of the presence of the Lord (39:2-3). Better than his father Jacob before him, he was stalwart in the recognition that to sin against the trust of a human relationship was to sin against God (39:9). Joseph may have had more than his share of egoism, but he also had a strong moral code which forbade his participation in lustful wickedness (39:9). He may have lost his garment but he refused to lose his innocence and fled from the scene of temptation (39:12).

In his relationship with his brothers it had been the lack of practical judgment which baited enmity, but in the trial by sensual pleasure it was the wisdom of practical action which preserved him. The experiences of life were gradually preparing Joseph for the fulfilment of his place in the covenant preservation.

The trial of confinement (*39:20-23*).—When the schemes of impure love are thwarted by righteous action, great fires sometimes are kindled, and it was so in the heart of Potiphar's wife. Joseph's righteousness condemned her, and so, for her own rational protection and for the purposes of revenge, she distorted the entire episode with a fictitious account and was the instrument of Joseph's confinement. The ancient action is as modern as today. Cruel actions are so often followed when people are thwarted in personal ambition. But God in his providence protects his own, and he protected Joseph.

The Preparation Through Dream Interpretation (40)

It is amazing how God can turn heartache into purposeful

service, but it is evident that the God of all sight was weaving each phase of Joseph's frustration into a preparatory tapestry. It was his presence in the prison which gave him the opportunity of dream interpretation for the butler and the baker. It was this which eventually opened the door for a place of honor and service in the kingdom.

The baker's dream simply increases the human interest element of the story, but the butler's dream paved the way for Joseph's restoration.

One has no difficulty in understanding how such dreams were possible for the baker and the butler. In their subliminal consciousness they no doubt had turned over and over the possibilities of their fate. Previous and present events no doubt gave some hint as to the possibility and probability with reference to their own restoration. In their hours of sleep, the minds kept working at the details with which they had labored in their conscious moments.

Joseph's ability to interpret the dreams speaks well of his close relationship to his God and his keen analysis of human personality and contemporary events. Each reinforced the other, and the two together gave him a message.

The Promotion to Influential Position (41)

Joseph's reputation from past days, the plight of the Egyptian nation, and the need of a plan for the meeting of the emergency were all contributing factors to Joseph's rise to power; but the over-all import of the scriptural context is that the co-ordinating factor in all of these was God. The Lord blessed Joseph's natural interest in events around him and used the knowledge gained thereby as the basis for revelation. Herein is true miracle. The dream of the fat and lean cattle is an appropriate dream for a Pharaoh bothered with the affairs of state. For a person as observant of "tides and times" as was Joseph, the interpretation did not seem too difficult, but for these events to coincide at the proper time to be of service in the preservation of the covenant people is "God's miracle" as timeless sovereign of the universe.

With the above as background, it may be proper to say that pleasing, personal traits on the part of Joseph made it, from the human standpoint, easier for him to find his place of service. His personal appearance was carefully pleasing (41:14), his personal faith was bold and daring in its reliance upon God (41:16), and his practical ambition was well geared for the moment (41:33). Realistically, such a statement as "let Pharaoh select a man discreet and wise" could hardly be considered as other than a reference to himself, for he had proved his superior ability. Perhaps there are times when, with proper humility, a man knows that God has prepared him as the man for the hour.

The fact that Joseph was given not only a signet ring and a golden necklace but also a wife from the Egyptian cult may indicate that in some sense he was to exercise both civil and religious authority in the supervision of plans for Egypt's grain bank program. At any rate, his was a place of high service which could count for both humanitarian and religious purposes. This is evidenced by the gift of the ring and the necklace.

The bestowal of the jewelry upon Joseph was quite in keeping with the inauguration of a person to the high office of vizier, or prime minister. In fact, there are many Egyptian texts which indicate that although the Pharaoh was the chief ruler of Egypt, he usually had a vizier serving under him, whose office actually served as the chief administrative center of the entire land.[3]

The Pharaoh delegated the administrative affairs of state to the prime minister, and he in turn apportioned the tasks to lesser officials immediately responsible to the prime minister.[4]

---

[3]George Steindorff and Keith C. Seele, *When Egypt Ruled the East* (Chicago: University of Chicago Press, 1942), p. 87.

[4]Pritchard, *op. cit.*, p. 212.

When the incumbent assumed his duties, he was properly installed by the Pharaoh himself, who gave a formal charge and dwelled at length upon the moral responsibilities involved in the office.[5] This would be in keeping with the above suggestion that Joseph's tasks had about them both humanitarian and religious qualities. Although from a period perhaps a bit later than the administration of Joseph, it is fortunate that numerous documents with reference to the office of prime minister have been preserved from the reign of Thutmose III (*ca.* 1490-1436 B.C.) Among the documents are texts dealing with the installation and duties of one Rekhmire who held such an office as did Joseph.[6]

A famine setting such as that which required the services of Joseph is attested also by Egyptian material. Numerous inscriptions speak of famine in the land, and some Egyptian tomb reliefs speak of the distribution of food to the needy. There is at least one Egyptian document which gives the tradition of seven lean years to be followed by seven years of plenty.[7] During such periods of famine, it was customary for Egypt to open her granaries to the aid of less fortunate outsiders. The custom of those from the outside visiting Egypt and borrowing from her granaries was known at least as early as the third dynasty of Egypt (2800 B.C.), for one text referring to that period reads, "The starvation year will have gone, and (people's) *borrowing* from their granaries will have departed."[8] The custom continued at least as late as the fourteenth century B.C., for a text from that period is inscribed: "That certain of the foreigners who know not how they may live have come. . . . Their countries are starving, and they are like the beasts of the desert."[9]

---

[5]Steindorff and Seele, *op. cit.*
[6]Pritchard, *op. cit.*, pp. 213 ff.
[7]*Ibid.*, p. 31.
[8]*Ibid.*, p. 32.
[9]*Ibid.*, p. 251.

One can thus understand the significance of Joseph's promotion to such an influential position and the benefit which such a position would enjoy in the blessing of the covenant group of Israel.

The Reunion of Joseph and His Brothers (42-45)

First Meeting in Egypt (42)

Few stories are more graphic in the portrayal of the lingering nature of sin than is the story of this reunion as told in chapter 42. A skilful and master narrator wove the material together. The tense atmosphere is shown by the furtive glances of the brothers (42:1). The searing guilt of a stained conscience (42:21) and the doctrine of recompense for evil (42:22,28) all contribute to the climax of sadness with which the chapter closes (42:36,38).

Along with the tense atmosphere which is set, there is at the same time the suggestion that the intervening years have brought some change in the attitude of the brothers. Every step of the trip to request food, the imprisonment of Simeon as hostage, and the surprise finding of the money in the sacks suggest that the brazen stubbornness of the younger years has mellowed into repentant remorse.

At any rate, the men claim this for themselves when they suggest to Joseph that they are *honest* men. Twice they used this word with reference to themselves (42:11,31), and twice it was used about them (42:19,33). This adjective *kenim* means "right, honest, stable, and steadfast." Perhaps its use is a conscious contrast with the rather unstable days of their younger years; its use indicates a contrast with a time when such a word could not express their character. Certainly there is a sense of guilt with reference to their sin against Joseph (42:21), and the sincerity of their changed attitude is expressed in their willingness to serve as ransom until their basic intent is proved (42:24,37).

Second Meeting in Egypt (43-44)

In the episode which transpired in the second visit to Egypt to acquire food, the true humility of the brothers is evident. Although at the banquet at Joseph's table Benjamin was fed five times more than the others and given a place of privilege, there is no indication at all that the brothers were jealous (43:34). It was a happy relationship which they shared with Benjamin, both because they had changed and, perhaps, because Benjamin had less pride and egoism than did Joseph during his younger days.

Humility and compassionate concern often go hand in hand, and such was true for the sons of Jacob, for they demonstrated anxious consideration for their father (44:20,29,34), a kind of concern which they had not had in those earlier years when they sold Joseph. Their sincerity of purpose was again demonstrated in that even though they must have felt that Benjamin was guilty, they were willing to suffer vicariously in his place (44:33).

Although these narratives are at no time interrupted by the author with a theological application to the covenant people, one wonders whether this was not the purpose involved in the transmission of the narratives. The attitudes and attributes presented are those which ought to be characteristic of a covenant group. Perhaps here is a subtle twofold presentation of expectation and denunciation in that so often these basic attitudes were lacking in Israel.

Reconciliation with the Brothers (45)

Although the story of the reunion is in itself quite fascinating, the theme underlying it is more important than the story itself. It is in this chapter that the theme of "God's perseverance in his plan" is climaxed. It is in the story of reunion and request for the father's presence that the true fitness of Joseph as a covenant leader, hinted earlier in the dreams of the bowing grain and stars (chap. 37), is shown.

Love, faith, and forgiveness are undergirded by the warm narrative. Joseph's genuine love, which expressed itself in forgiveness toward his brothers, is evident in the genuine display of emotion which gripped him (45:1-2). It was Joseph who took the action necessary to repair the breach— another evidence of his forgiving spirit. He was a paragon of charity in his abstinence from personal criticism; their guilt had brought the pain of self-criticism. But a charitable and forgiving spirit is possible when one has such a faith in the providence of God as did Joseph (45:5). He knew that God had overruled and used their evil intention so that it turned out to be a blessing.

The sojourn in Egypt, initiated originally by the trickery of the brothers, actually served to preserve Jacob and his family from famine. It provided a background for the acquirement of things of value as a cultural heritage. The exposure to Egyptian law certainly prepared them for that day when they would need a law of their own. In a rudimentary way, it provided initial seed of stability for being molded into a nation. Even the persecution of the Egyptian sojourn served to strengthen the ties of kinship and sympathy.

But it is on a personal note related to Jacob, and not Joseph, that the narrative ends. When Jacob heard that his son Joseph was alive, he stopped the recital of grandeur and gifts. It was enough for him that Joseph was alive. As Skinner has suggested, "The psychology of old age could not be more sympathetically or convincingly treated."[10]

Settlement of the United Family in Egypt (46:1 to 47:26)

Jacob's Journey to Egypt and Settlement in Goshen (46:1 to 47:12)

It is evident that the troubled years of Jacob's life had

---

[10]Skinner, *op. cit.*, p. 490.

culminated in times of introspection and reflection. He had learned much and was considerably wiser and more spiritually mature; and so when the challenge came to move to Egypt, he went at God's command (46:1-7). The move to Egypt presented quite a contrast. He started his career by journeying *without* God, but ended it by journeying *with* God (46:2).

Indeed, it is the religious note about the move to Egypt which is so striking. To be sure, chapter 46 is a compilation from the three basic sources, *J, E,* and *P.* However, it is in the fairly early *E* source that mention is made of the covenant purpose in connection with the Egyptian sojourn (46:3). It may be that the written source had formalized the hope in later literary dress, but there must have been handed down some oral tradition about Jacob's covenant hopes in connection with this move to Egypt. Perhaps Jacob saw it as an opportunity to stabilize his family, get it on its feet and implant some impresssions about God's use of their lives, which all too often they had forgotten.

The providence of God is such a constant theme in the entire Joseph narrative, chapters 37-50, that the guiding hand of God for covenant fulfilment is certainly not out of order in chapter 46. One might ask how much of this was recognized through the look of retrospection. No doubt, much of the recognition of God's will and purpose was perceived through the recounting of the places over which their steps had taken them. This is the normal way of becoming certain about God's will. But this is encouraging. Although man cannot always perceive at the moment that God is at work in his redemptive purpose, his reflection upon the pattern of events in the past will encourage him to keep faith in the sovereignty of God until such time as an opportunity of retrospection can put the pieces of the puzzle in clearer perspective.

Some attention will be given to the descendants of Jacob in connection with chapter 49, but, in passing, a word with reference to chapter 46:8-27 may be helpful.

The list of people who went with Jacob into Egypt is not intended to be an accurate list of Jacob's sons or grandsons. It is more or less a general description of the relatives of Jacob, from whom seventy leading clans developed, and roughly corresponds to Numbers 26:5 ff. Testimony that it is not intended to be a specifically accurate list but rather a vehicle to emphasize God's blessing of the people in the growth of a nation is evident in the failure to list Er and Onan and in its inclusion of Joseph and his kinsmen who actually did not accompany Jacob into Egypt but were already there.

That there were various traditions is manifested in the Acts 7:14 speech of Stephen, in which he quoted or paraphrased this section and used the number seventy-five rather than seventy. To be sure, he was using the Septuagint tradition which includes five names at the end of the English verse 20 which are omitted in the Hebrew text.

An example of Hebrew practice in indicating relationships may be found in Genesis 46:22, where fourteen "sons" are attributed to Rachel, in contrast to the two sons named elsewhere. It is common knowledge that the Hebrew term *ben* is a loose term which may simply indicate "sons," "kinsfolk," or "descendants," another indication that there is no effort here to be numerically accurate in Jacob's list. It is the Priestly source which is used for portraying this genealogical table, and it is common knowledge that the priestly writer used such lists as literary vehicles for presenting the blessing of God. To the Hebrew mind, an increase in number meant increase in blessing.

Unfortunately, it has been impossible to find the name "Goshen" (46:28) in Egyptian records. A name which once was so identified was done so by mistake. This same area, however, was called "the land of Rameses" (47:11) and the "field of Zoan" (Psalm 78:12). The latter of the two names occurs often in Egyptian records. The area was blessed by a thirty-to-forty-mile valley which connected the Nile with

Lake Timsah. The region was abundantly rich and fertile and at times produced more revenue and sustained more flocks and herds than any other place in the entire land.

It was a good place for Jacob to settle,[11] and Jacob was duly grateful, as implied by the term "bless" in 47:7. The term is *y°varek*, which implies good wishes which arise from a heart of gratitude and appreciation. This humbled and appreciative Jacob is certainly a different man from the trick-ster who years before in selfish ambition had deceived his brother and his father. This contrast of attitudes is further heightened in Pharaoh's question, "How many are the days of the years of your life?" (47:8, RSV). He noted that Jacob looked old, although, as compared with the other patriarchs, he really was not. The question cut the conscience of Jacob, for he knew that for him life had been a pilgrimage and that he often had filled the journey with evil, making it much harder.

Joseph's Agrarian Policy (47:13-26)

The covenant promise was a promise to bless for the purpose of being a blessing, and nowhere is the physical phase of "being a blessing" more evident than in Joseph's service to varied people during the hour of famine.

There has been much criticism of the land policy which Joseph inaugurated for the feeding of hungry people. Of course, the policy included the placing of all lands in the hands of government ownership.

The people worked the land for the government, kept 80 per cent of the returns for themselves and gave 20 per cent of all returns as a tax to Pharaoh. This really was a very con-siderate and lenient policy. According to J. H. Breasted, the authoritative Egyptologist, up until Joseph's time, the land in all probability had been in the hands of a few rich noblemen

---

[11]Wright, *Biblical Archaeology*, p. 56.

who operated on the basis of the plantation system with serfs or slaves doing the work.[12]   The common people had little land control, so what Joseph actually did was to put the land back under the supervision of the masses.   The people themselves seem to have thought that it was a splendid arrangement (47:25).   When one realizes the large share which a modern government absorbs in taxes, the equity of Joseph's plan will be understood.

In addition to the biblical record, Egyptian records indicate that such a plan as recorded here was in effect after the expulsion of the Hyksos from Egypt.   At that time, lands and fields were the property of the state. Only the temples possessed free property.[13]

The Parting of the Way: Death and Burial of Jacob and Joseph (47:27 to 50:26)

In this last section it is utterly impossible and useless to make any attempt at the establishment of a definite chronology. The sources are used without any effort at strict harmonization. For instance, a picture of the death of Jacob (47:31)[14] is followed by an account of the blessing of Joseph and Jacob's sons (48-49), with the death reported again after the blessing (49:33b).[15] It is evident that the inspired compiler was more interested in giving as many details as possible than he was in harmonization.   As long as his purpose is realized, there is no difficulty.

The Blessings (47:27 to 49:33)

Literary considerations.—In preparation for the last instructions to Joseph and for his will and testament, Jacob asked that Joseph's hand be placed under his thigh (47:29).   This was similar to a very ancient custom, older than the Hebrews, of

---

[12]Breasted, *op. cit.*, p. 169.
[13]Steindorff and Seele, *op. cit.*, p. 88.
[14]Yahwistic source.
[15]Priestly source.

making an oath by putting the hands upon the genital organs as symbols of life-giving power, power which would enable an oath to be kept.[16] The Jewish teachers Ibn Ezra, Rashi, and Sforno suggest that the person who gave an oath was accustomed to holding something sacred in his hand. Circumcision was a basic precept of the covenant and had come to Jacob through exceeding pain. Placing the hand in the vicinity of the circumcision perhaps implied a passing on of covenant consciousness and covenant responsibility.[17] Ibn Ezra called attention to a custom known in India which specified that an individual would place his hand under the covenant maker's thigh and the latter would sit upon the hand. This represented an agreement on the part of the recipient to carry out the covenant.[18] With this formal oath, Ephraim and Manasseh, the two sons of Joseph, were adopted as covenant sons (chap. 48). This explains why there is no tribe of Joseph among the twelve tribes; the two replace Joseph.

It is generally agreed that the core of the Genesis 49 speech on the future of the tribes is one of the oldest pieces of Hebrew poetry. That there must have been some historic setting such as the deathbed blessing by Jacob, it is agreed. It was a common custom to make a valedictory address shortly before death. However, in its present form, the poem is a product of the compilation and editing of later years. It is interesting to note that the pattern of history outlined for each of the tribes is that which they followed. Jacob had observed the people involved long enough to know the basic tenets of their character and the probable outcome of their lives. In this sense, much of the poem is prediction. On the other hand, some of the material is so similar to that of other sections of the Old Testament (cf. Deut. 33; Judg. 5) that it is to be suspected that some of the material is in the nature of later additions

---

[16]Simpson, *op. cit.*, p. 652.
[17]Cohen, *op. cit.*, p. 122.
[18]*Ibid.*

as an eponymous history, perhaps unfolded, as Skinner suggests, during the time of the Judges and the initial stages of the monarchy.[19] Further considerations suggest an atmosphere of lateness about the final editing. The poem is possessed of a strong national sentiment which hardly could have been true in Jacob's own age, for they were not yet a nation. The subjects of the oracles do not seem to be Jacob's sons as individuals but as tribes.[20]

The arrangement of the chapter lends itself to the consideration of three groups—the sons of Leah, the sons of the handmaidens, and the sons of Rachel, although no chronological order is followed; otherwise some of the children of the handmaidens would have been listed immediately after Judah. The only possibility of a chronological listing here according to birth is that lists given elsewhere simply group the sons with reference to their mothers and contain no thought for age.

Before trying to delineate some of the characteristics implied for the various tribes, however, it is necessary to stress again the historical setting of an oral blessing, such as that which Jacob is giving here and which Isaac gave on an earlier occasion. The Nuzi tablets, from the Mesopotamian period of the middle of the second millennium B.C., contain a ceremony for adoption, probably a similar ceremony to that by which Jacob adopted Joseph's sons,[21] and the same tablets represent the legitimacy of oral blessings and even report a case where an oral blessing was substantiated in court.[22] Although the blessings are now in a composite form, their historical setting must be remembered. Had there been no tradition that Jacob gave a blessing, the present material would have been worthless.

From the literary standpoint, it has been suggested that

---

[19]Skinner, *op. cit.*, p. 508.
[20]*Ibid.*
[21]Pritchard, *op. cit.*, pp. 219 ff.
[22]Wright, *Biblical Archaeology*, p. 44.

many of the very difficult passages in the blessing are actually
a play upon words whereby the author either is saying two
things at once or is saying one thing and insinuating another.[23]
One only has to recall the vision of summer fruit (Amos 8:1-2)
or the rod of the almond vision (Jer. 1:11-12) to realize that
such plays upon words were not uncommon in the very literary
period to which much of chapter 49 is to be dated, since it
seems to be composed of the Yahwistic and Priestly sources.
Peters' reconstruction or play upon words is of necessity
based upon the unpointed Hebrew text.[24] The reader will
want to remember that there were no vowel points until the
time of Masoretes, in the realm of the sixth to the ninth centuries. Certainly there is truth in the supposition of a play
upon words in the blessing. But perhaps Peters pays too little
attention to the traditional Masoretic readings and casts them
aside with too little, if any, evidence.

Tribal characterization.—49:3-4. Reuben, pictured as the
unstable one, had good possibilities but did not use them
wisely. Although he possessed qualities for good, through
wrong action or lack of action, he turned them into evil.

The theft of Bilhah, his father's concubine (Gen. 35:22),
perhaps was indicative of his desire to have the leadership of
the tribes, since the possession of the ruler's concubine generally indicated the right to rule. He, as the first-born son, tried to
usurp a right which would have in time been his anyway. On
the other hand, he failed to earn the right to lead because of
his delaying tactics in times which demanded action.

He is chastised in the song of Deborah because his heart
was possessed of fear and he tarried among the sheepfolds
when the call was sounded for war (Judg. 5:15-16). This
loss of heart was followed not only by a loss of eminence but,
according to Detueronomy, by a loss of size (Deut. 33:6).

---

[23]J. P. Peters, "Jacob's Blessing," *Journal of Biblical Literature* (June, 1886),
p. 99.
[24]*Ibid.*

There may have been population loss by war and natural causes, but perhaps some of the more stalwart of the Reuben group united with other tribal elements. Perhaps the tribal history might best be summarized in the phrase "Pride goeth before destruction" (cf. Gen. 49:3b).

49:5-7. Comrades of evil were the brothers Simeon and Levi. Tradition pictured these two as the instigators in the plot against Joseph, and, of course, these two were the avengers in the Dinah episode with the Shechemites (Gen. 34).

Whether the two evil partners eventually turned against each other is not known, but this may have been a partial cause of their settlement in two separate sections of the country, Simeon in the South and Levi in the North. Since Simeon is completely omitted in the blessing of Moses (Deut. 33) and in the song of Deborah (Judg. 5), this group may have been assimilated into, and swallowed by, the people of Judah at an early date. There seems to be some intimation of this in the land allotment of Joshua 19:1 (cf. Gen. 49:7). Testimony of such assimilation seems to be given by a comparison of the two census lists in Numbers 1 and Numbers 26. The second census represents a larger decrease in size than that of any of the other tribes. This separation between Simeon and Levi was a blessing, for it allowed Levi to exhibit ultimately some good qualities, which allowed his people to become the priestly tribe.

49:8-12. Perhaps no other part of the poem is so typical of later editorializing as this one on Judah, the lionhearted. No doubt the leadership qualities of Judah were recognized by Jacob and others at an early date. Perhaps this recognition was blessed with the spiritual insight that God had something unusual planned for this group. Even so, one can feel the pride of the Yahwistic writer as he wrote about and magnified this very group from which he himself was descended.

The brothers recognized the stronger qualities in Judah when they paid heed to his mediating voice in their treatment of Joseph (Gen. 37:26), and something of the magnanimity of Judah's character is displayed in his willingness to serve as ransom for Benjamin (Gen. 44). Perhaps it is because of this contrast in the later actions of Judah with his earlier violation of the rights of Tamar, his daughter-in-law (Gen. 38), that someone has characterized him as the repentant son.

A glaring difficulty in the blessing upon Judah is gained by simply placing together the King James and the Revised Standard translations of verse 10. "The sceptre shall not depart from Judah, nor a lawgiver from between his feet, until Shiloh come" (KJV). "The scepter shall not depart from Judah, nor the ruler's staff from between his feet, until he comes to whom it belongs" (RSV).

Admittedly, the Hebrew will allow either reading and, probably, the King James' reading involves less necessity for linguistic scrutiny. But even to early interpreters, who allowed "Shiloh" to stand as a proper name, there was no certainty as to what it meant. Ultimately, the Talmud and later medieval rabbis took the name to be a messianic title. Others sought to avoid the problem by translating it "until he [Judah] comes to Shiloh," thus, inferring that Judah would rule as a great people in Shiloh. In addition to the fact that this event did not occur, such a reading improperly manipulates the Hebrew construction, for there is nothing to indicate a preposition, or "direction towards" Shiloh, nor is Shiloh very significant on a permanent basis, for it apparently was destroyed by the Philistines during the last phase of the period of the judges. The Revised Standard reading seems nearer the original intention of the passage. The Hebrew word שִׁילֹה is probably a poetic abbreviation of the two Hebrew words אֲשֶׁר and לֹו, "which" and "to him." Thus, the literal reading is "until he comes, which to him," or "until he comes to whom it belongs."

The scepter (*shevet*) mentioned in the first part of the verse is a sign of kingly authority and so is the word for staff (*mechoqeq*). Thus, the passage would seem to indicate a belief that the tribe of Judah would continue to exist until its scepter and staff were taken over by someone else, an individual.

This interpretation is buttressed by the fact that the phrase is translated as "until he come whose right it is" (Ezek. 21:27). Thus, the passage, may simply be a testimony for the personal pre-eminence of a ruler from Judah, such as David, and gives more authority for the greatness of the Davidic dynasty. To be sure, it would be so used by the lineage of Judah. However, it is impossible to forget that Judah was alive as an entity at the time of the Messiah, and the messianic principle which anticipated a messiah from an early period must have been a dual implication of the phrase.[25]

49:14-15. Although their work was of a different sort, the territory of Zebulun lay next to Issachar's, so they have come to be known traditionally as fellow workmen. At least a portion of his time, Zebulun joined with his coastal neighbor, Asher, in the region of Sidon (Phoenicia) and worked hard at seafaring. Issachar dwelled inland between the Great Plain and the Jordan and perhaps valued the imports which Zebulun shared in return for the fruit of the soil gathered by hard toil.

It would seem that Issachar found it difficult to maintain independence and from time to time was captured by others and had to serve as a slave, the meaning of the term *sebel* used in verse 15. Some disfavor was directed toward the people of Issachar by the other tribes, for Issachar apparently preferred submission with a "handout" from a foreign master rather than heroic exertion and freedom. These people were not willing to pay the price which manhood required (cf. Gen. 49:14). Actually, one learns from the correspondence of the

---

[25]This is in contrast to the view of Sigmund Mowinckel in *He That Cometh*, in which he views the Messiah as a development growing out of the failure of the monarchy. Needless to say, it is also in contrast to the suggestion, sometimes given, that the subject of the verb is, by ellipsis, Jeroboam and that the passage refers to a Northern revolt against Judean supremacy.

Amarna period (fourteenth century B.C.) that the territory which Issachar occupied was from time-to-time used as an area from which to draw forced labor for people living in the region of Megiddo.[26] Because of an apparent willingness to perform service for the Canaanites, rather than vice versa as the covenant anticipated, Issachar gained a poor reputation in the annals of history. Since the name "Issachar" means "laborer," it may be a nickname given later to a people originally called by another appellation.[27]

49:16-18. The comment upon Dan, the shrewd one is evidence that children whose lineage was traced to a handmaiden received an inheritance even as did those of full parentage. The subtle nature of the Danites was illustrated in their attack upon the Sidonians (Judg. 18:7 ff.). Although a weak tribe, their craftiness won for them a place in the historical annals. There was nothing about Dan which exhibited concern for true religion. This may be the reason that in the New Testament use of the tribal names as symbols of the followers of God (Rev. 7), the name of Dan is missing.

49:19-21. Gad, the fearless, although often attacked, was fortunate to make such counterattacks as to maintain freedom. This constant oppression at the hands of others prepared them to sympathize with the less fortunate (cf. 1 Chron. 12:8; 2 Sam. 17:27).

Asher, the happy, settled the fertile strip above Mt. Carmel and, apparently, became rich from the oil for which the region was famous (cf. Deut. 33:24). However, Asher actually made little contribution to the national life of Israel and probably compromised its covenant responsibility for personal gain. Of Asher it is said that the Asherites dwelt among the Canaanites (Judg. 1:32), whereas, of the other tribes it is said that the Canaanites dwelt among them.

---

[26]Pritchard, *op. cit.*, p. 485.
[27]Martin Noth, *The History of Israel* (London: A. & C. Black, Ltd., 1958), p. 66.

Gad and Asher had wealth of a material kind, but Naphtali, the inspiring one, seemed to care less about the material and majored more upon true wisdom and joy. This in turn ennobled character and inspired many. Here is a trait which would aid a covenant group to win friends and influence people.

49:22-26. The description here of Joseph, the "fruitful bough," is really a summary of the life and character of Joseph as it has been presented in the book of Genesis and, therefore, probably contains material more closely approximating the actual speech of Jacob than do the other blessings. He was mistreated (v. 23), but God's providence prevailed and Joseph remained strong (vv. 24-25). The language used is that of an early period, for mention of the breasts and wombs as symbols of blessing is to be found in the Ras Shamra material.[28] On the other hand, verse 26 perhaps represents the sentiment of a later period and is commending the northern leadership in its efforts at establishing a strong monarchy.

49:27. Although a precious son to Jacob, Benjamin, the wolf, had little part to play in the religious phase of covenant history and receives only passing mention. When there had been opportunity for greatness, such as in the period of Saul, it was spoiled. Perhaps the early days of favoritism and the tradition of such, which extended from the time of Jacob, made Benjamin so greedy for gain and attention that the tribe became the victim of hereditary and environmental weakness.

Zodiac signs.—It is not basic to the purpose of this author to attempt any tracing of relationship between the twelve tribes and the signs of the zodiac, the imaginary path of the moon and planets and the sun's path, marked by twelve divisions and represented by twelve symbols. However, it is of such interest as to demand recognition that there are some similarities between the names and characteristics of the tribes and the symbols of the zodiac.

The history of the zodiac extends back at least to the time

---

[28]Wright, *Biblical Archaeology,* p. 109.

of Hammurabi,[29] when there were sixteen symbols, later reduced to twelve. The fact that there were twelve tribes, the same number as the zodiac symbols, and the fact that the symbols of some of the tribes were the same as zodiac signs,[30] may suggest that, poetically, the writer of Genesis is suggesting that these were the fates of the covenant people as "fixed" in the heavens. There was something God-ordained about their fate. It was the ordained outcome for people of their character. That the Genesis compiler was aware of zodiac symbolism is perhaps further suggested in the dream of Joseph, when, sun, moon, and stars (zodiac figures) paid obeisance.[31] Is this a further symbol that the God of the heavens had ordained the primacy of Joseph?

At any rate, it is very evident from the blessing that people of every walk of life, with widely varying characteristics, were to carry out the covenant witness. But it is also evident from the attention given to repentant Judah and faithful Joseph that the covenant instruments most blessed are those characterized by repentance and faith.

The Deaths (50)

Both Jacob and Joseph were embalmed (Gen. 50:2,26), a custom of regular practice in Egypt and the normal way for preparing the body of an important person for burial.[32] Since the custom was reserved normally for persons of recognized stature, the embalming of Jacob may be an indication that he too, along with his son, eventually won great favor in Egypt.

The *Tale of Sinuhe*, perhaps a bit earlier than the Joseph period, tells the story of an Egyptian who did not wish to be buried on foreign soil and who was allowed the privilege of burial in his homeland after his body was prepared with

---

[29]Voegelin, *op. cit.*, p. 30.

[30]"Water bearer," (49:4); Leo (49:9); Ass (49:14); Serpent (49:17); Archer (49:23-24); Wolf (49:27). Cf. Voegelin, *op. cit.*, p. 31.

[31]Voegelin, *op. cit.*, p. 35.

[32]Wright, *Biblical Archaeology*, p. 54.

ointments and wrappings.[33]   It was only natural that Jacob
(Gen. 49:29) and Joseph (Gen. 50:25) should desire to be
buried in the land which formed part of the covenant promise.

The death of Joseph at the age of one hundred and ten may
be seen as a further link with the Egyptian background out
of which the Joseph narrative comes rather than a literal figure
for his age.   The age of one hundred and ten was a common
symbol in Egyptian literature as the traditional length of a
happy and prosperous life.[34]   God had been gracious.

Even a chapter devoted primarily to death has an underlying
theme of covenant providence and covenant faith.   The statement of verse 20 is a fitting statement of God's providence in
the perpetuation of a covenant people.   "As for you, you
meant evil against me; but God meant it for good, to bring
it about that many people should be kept alive, as they are
today."   No less challenging is the statement of faith implied
in the belief expressed in verse 24 that one day this preserved
people would go up to possess one covenant place, the land
of Canaan.   Thus, the book closes on a note which more or
less summarizes the theme of the book, the promise of God to
prepare a people as an instrument of redemption and to give
them a place on which, and from which, the drama of reconciliation could be enacted.

Conclusion

The author prefers to call the approach used here the
"theological approach to the book of Genesis." While it uses the
fruit of critical research, it has due reverence for the message
of the Bible.   Indeed, the purpose is to help to discover the
message of the book of Genesis, not as science or history, but
as religion.   Allowances have been made for the human aspects
of the record.   This, at times, has necessitated an effort to

---

[33]Pritchard, *op. cit.*, pp. 19 ff.
[34]*Ibid.*, p. 414.

ascertain the age and order of the various traditions. But through them as they presently are, there often breathes the spirit of God to make them, not just words, but the living Word.

It will have been noticed that two main themes have come into focus, namely, man's need and God's answer to man's need. While the need of man is emphasized from several different perspectives in Genesis 1-11, God's answer involves the dual facts of election and covenant. While some scholars regard the emphasis upon the covenant as a rewriting of the Abrahamic history from the Mosaic standpoint, the suggestion has little validity. Nearly all will agree, even as the biblical narrative states, that because of his innate sense of personal election, Abraham made a contribution in the initiation of God's plan of redemption. Election always implies covenant, for one is elected *to* something and *for* something. Any later editing tended only to heighten and place emphasis upon the doctrines of election and covenant already present.

It is a long trek from Abraham and Ur in Mesopotamia to Joseph and Egypt. The many stops, minor and major incidents, and the "side" stories, which have a direct and indirect connection with the main theme, all serve their purpose in the larger emphasis that God chose human instruments through whom to work. These instruments were possessed of the same human frailties which beset the servants of God today. Thus, one better understands the predicaments which slowed their stewardship and, yet, at the same time, underlined the perseverance and providence of God in the attainment of his goal.

The fact that an Abraham, an Isaac, a Jacob, or a Joseph could have the weaknesses of human flesh and yet be used for the purposes of God gives encouragement and comfort and hope for service to the man in the pew today. On the other hand, these same frailties cause one to realize that those initially used in the plan of redemption are really signposts pointing to human deficiency and the need for a stronger mediator of a better and more sure covenant. What the covenant people failed to do, the true Suffering Servant did. But how much clearer one sees the principles upon which he worked and works if he sees them in seedbed form in the Old Testament. Jesus fulfils in *fact* and *faith* what in the old covenant was enunciated in hope. Genesis makes a contribution to the understanding of the need, the hope, and the faith!

Bibliography

ALBRIGHT, WILLIAM FOXWELL. *From the Stone Age to Christianity.* 2d ed. Garden City: Doubleday & Co., Inc., 1957.

————. *Recent Discoveries in Bible Lands.* New York: Funk & Wagnalls Co., 1936.

ALLEMAN, HERBERT C., and FLACK, ELMER E., *Old Testament Commentary.* Philadelphia: The Muhlenberg Press, 1948.

BARNETT, LINCOLN. "The Dawn of Religion," *Life,* XXXIX (December 12, 1955), 76-91,95-96.

BARTH, KARL. *The Epistle to the Romans.* Translated by EDWYN C. HOSKYNS. London: Oxford University Press, 1933.

BENNETT, W. H. (ed.). *Genesis.* Vol. I: *The New Century Bible.* Edinburgh: T. C. & E. C. Jack, n.d.

BENTZEN, AAGE. *Introduction to the Old Testament.* 2 vols. 2d ed. Copenhagen: G. E. C. Gads Forlag, 1952.

BONHOEFFER, DIETRICH. *Creation and Fall.* Translated by JOHN C. FLETCHER. New York: Macmillan Co., 1959.

BOWMAN, JOHN WICK. *Prophetic Realism and the Gospel.* Philadelphia: Westminster Press, 1945.

BREASTED, JAMES HENRY. *A History of Egypt.* 2d ed. New York: Charles Scribner's Sons, 1909.

BROWN, FRANCIS, DRIVER, S. R., and BRIGGS, CHARLES A. *A Hebrew and English Lexicon of the Old Testament.* Oxford: Clarendon Press, 1952.

BRUNNER, EMIL. *Revelation and Reason.* Translated by OLIVE WYON. London: Student Christian Movement Press, Ltd., 1947.

BUCHANAN, GEORGE WESLEY. "The Old Testament Meaning of the Knowledge of Good and Evil," *Journal of Biblical Literature,* LXXV (June, 1956), 114-120.

CHRISTIAN, W. A. "Augustine on the Creation of the World," *Harvard Theological Review,* XLVI (January, 1953), 1-26.

CLAPP, FREDERICK G. "Geology and Bitumens of the Dead Sea

Area, Palestine and Transjordan," *The Bulletin of the American Association of Petroleum Geologists*, XX (1936), 881-909. (Quoted by J. Pemose Harland in "The Destruction of the Cities of the Plain," *The Biblical Archaeologist*, VI (September, 1943), 49.

COHEN, A. (ed.). *The Soncino Chumash*. London: Soncino Press, Ltd., 1947.

Courier-Journal (Louisville), November 14, 1957.

CUNLIFFE-JONES, H. *The Authority of the Biblical Revelation*. London: James Clarke & Co., Ltd., 1945.

DAUBE, DAVID, and YARON, REUVEN. "Jacob's Reception by Laban," *The Journal of Semitic Studies*, I (January, 1956), 60-62.

DAVIDSON, A. B. *Hebrew Syntax*. 3rd ed. Edinburgh: T. & T. Clark, 1912.

———. *The Theology of the Old Testament*. Edinbrugh: T. & T. Clark, 1904.

DEANE, WILLIAM J. *Abraham: His Life and Times*. London: James Nisbet & Co., Ltd., n.d.

DEISSMANN, ADOLF. *Bible Studies*. Edinburgh: T. & T. Clark, 1901.

DODS, MARCUS. "The Book of Genesis." *The Expositor's Bible*. London: Hodder & Stoughton, 1891.

DOWEY, EDWARD A., JR. *The Knowledge of God in Calvin's Theology*. New York: Columbia University Press, 1952.

DRIVER, S. R. *The Book of Genesis*. London: Methuen & Co., Ltd., 1911.

———. *Sermons on Subjects Connected with the Old Testament*. London: Methuen & Co., Ltd., 1892.

EICHRODT, WALTER. *Theologie des Alten Testamenta*. Vol. II. Berlin: Evangelische Verlagsastalt, 1950.

FILSON, FLOYD. "Method in Studying Biblical History," *Journal of Biblical Literature*, LXIX (March, 1950).

FINEGAN, JACK. *Light from the Ancient Past*. Princeton: Princeton University Press, 1946.

FRAZER, JAMES GEORGE. *Folk-Lore in the Old Testament*. 3 vols. London: Macmillan & Co., Ltd., 1919.

Gesenius' Hebrew and Chaldee Lexicon. Translated by SAMUEL PRIDEAUX TREGELLES. Grand Rapids: Wm. B. Eerdman's Publishing Co., 1957.

GLUECK, NELSON. *The River Jordan.* Philadelphia: Westminster Press, 1946.

GORDON, CYRUS H. "Abraham and the Merchants of Ura," *The Journal of Near Eastern Studies,* XVII (January, 1958), 28-31.

———. *The World of the Old Testament.* Garden City: Doubleday & Co., Inc., 1958.

GOTTWALD, NORMAN K. *A Light to the Nations.* New York: Harper & Bros., 1959.

GUNKEL, HERMANN. *The Legends of Genesis.* Translated by W. H. CARRUTH. Chicago: Open Court, 1901.

HASTINGS, JAMES (ed.). *The Greater Men and Women of the Bible.* Edinburgh: T. & T. Clark, 1913.

HAURET, CHARLES. *Beginnings: Genesis and Modern Science.* Translated by E. P. EMMANS, Dubuque: The Priory Press, 1955.

HOFTIZER, J. "Some Remarks to the Tale of Noah's Drunkenness," *Studies on the Book of Genesis.* ("Oudtestamentische Studiën," XII) Leiden: E. J. Brill, 1958.

HOOKE, S. H. "In the Beginning," *The Clarendon Bible.* Oxford: Clarendon Press, 1947.

———. *The Siege Perilous.* London: Student Christian Movement Press, Ltd., 1956.

JACOB, EDMOND. *Theology of the Old Testament.* Translated by ARTHUR W. HEATHCOTE and PHILIP J. ALLCOCK. London: Hodder & Stoughton, 1958.

KEIL, C. F., and DELITZSCH, F. *The Pentateuch.* Vol. I: *Biblical Commentary on the Old Testament.* Translated by JAMES MARTIN. Grand Rapids: Wm. B. Eerdman's Publishing Co., 1951.

KIERKEGAARD, SÖREN. Fear and Trembling. Translated by ROBERT PAYNE. London: Oxford University Press, 1939.

KNIGHT, GEORGE A. F. *A Christian Theology of the Old Testament.* Richmond: John Knox Press, 1959.

KÖHLER, LUDWIG. *Old Testament Theology.* Translated by A. S. TODD. Philadelphia: Westminster Press, 1953.

LEWIS, C. S. *The Screwtape Letters.* London: Geoffrey Bles, Ltd., 1942.

MEYER, F. B. *Abraham or, The Obedience of Faith.* London: Morgan & Scott, Ltd., 1911.

MOWINCKEL, SIGMUND. *The Old Testament As Word of God.* Translated by REIDER B. BJORNARD. New York: Abingdon Press, 1959.

MURTONEN, A. "The Fixation in Writing of Various Parts of the Pentateuch," *Vetus Testamentum,* III (January, 1953), 46-53.

NIELSEN, EDUARD. *Oral Tradition.* Chicago: Alec R. Allenson, Inc., 1954.

NOTH, MARTIN. *The History of Israel.* London: Adam and Charles Black, 1958.

NYBERG, H. S. *Studien zum Hoseabuche, Zugleich ein Beitrag zur Klaerung des Problems der Altestamentlichen Textkritik.* Uppsala Universitets Arsskrift, 1935.

ORLINSKY, HARRY M. "The Plain Meaning of Ru^{a}h in Gen. 1:2," *The Jewish Quarterly Review,* XLVIII (October, 1957), 174-182.

OTTLEY, ROBERT LAURENCE. *Aspects of the Old Testament.* London: Longmans, Green & Co., Ltd., 1897.

PETERS, J. P. "Jacob's Blessing," *Journal of Biblical Literature* (June, 1886), p. 99.

PFEIFFER, ROBERT H. *Introduction to the Old Testament.* New York: Harper & Bros., 1948.

PIETERS, ALBERTUS. *Notes on Genesis.* Vol. I. Grand Rapids: Wm. B. Eerdman's Publishing Co., 1954.

POPE, LISTON. *The Kingdom Beyond Caste.* New York: Friendship Press, 1957.

PRITCHARD, JAMES B. (ed.). *Ancient Near Eastern Texts.* 2d ed. Princeton: Princeton University Press, 1955.

RAMM, BERNARD. *The Christian View of Science and Scripture.* Grand Rapids: Wm. B. Eerdman's Publishing Co., 1955.

RICHARDSON, ALAN. *Genesis I-XI.* London: Student Christian Movement Press, Ltd., 1953.

ROBINSON, H. WHEELER. *Inspiration and Revelation in the Old Testament.* Oxford: Clarendon Press, 1946.

ROWLEY, H. H. *The Servant of the Lord and Other Essays on the Old Testament.* London: Lutterworth Press, 1952.

SAMPEY, JOHN R. *The Heart of the Old Testament.* Nashville: Broadman Press, 1922.

SCHWEITZER, GEORGE K. "The Origin of the Universe," *Review and Expositor,* LIV (April, 1957), 178-194.

SIMPSON, C. A. "The Book of Genesis," *The Interpreter's Bible*. Edited by NOLAN B. HARMON. New York: Abingdon-Cokesbury Press, 1952. Vol. I.

SKINNER, JOHN. *A Critical and Exegetical Commentary on Genesis*. Vol. I of *The International Critical Commentaries*. Edited by SAMUEL DRIVER, ALFRED PLUMMER, and CHARLES BRIGGS. Edinburgh: T. & T. Clark, 1910.

SMITH, T. C. *Jesus in the Gospel of John*. Nashville: Broadman Press, 1959.

STEINDORFF, GEORGE, and SEELE, KEITH C. *When Egypt Ruled the East*. Chicago: University of Chicago Press, 1942.

THOMAS, W. H. GRIFFITH. *Through the Pentateuch Chapter by Chapter*. Grand Rapids: Wm. B. Eerdman's Publishing Co., 1957.

TILLICH, PAUL. *Systematic Theology*. 2 vols. Chicago: University of Chicago Press, 1951.

TOYNBEE, ARNOLD. *An Historian's Approach to Religion*. London: Oxford University Press, 1956.

VOEGELIN, ERIC. *Israel and Revelation*. "Order and History." Vol. I. Baton Rouge: La. State University Press, 1956.

VRIEZEN, TH. C. *An Outline of Old Testament Theology*. Oxford: Basil Blackwell, 1958.

WOOLLEY, SIR LEONARD. *Abraham*. London: Faber & Faber, Ltd., 1936.

WRIGHT, G. ERNEST. *Biblical Archaeology*. Philadelphia: Westminster Press, 1957.

————. *The Old Testament Against Its Environment*. "Studies In Biblical Theology." No. 2. Chicago: Alec R. Allenson, Inc., 1950.